ADAM CLAYTON
POWELL, JR.

ADAM CLAYTON POWELL, JR.

Robert E. Jakoubek

Senior Consulting Editor
Nathan Irvin Huggins
Director
W.E.B. Du Bois Institute for Afro-American Research
Harvard University

CHELSEA HOUSE PUBLISHERS
New York   Philadelphia

Editor-in-Chief Nancy Toff
Executive Editor Remmel T. Nunn
Managing Editor Karyn Gullen Browne
Copy Chief Juliann Barbato
Picture Editor Adrian G. Allen
Art Director Giannella Garrett
Manufacturing Manager Gerald Levine

Staff for ADAM CLAYTON POWELL, JR:
Senior Editor Richard Rennert
Associate Editor Perry King
Assistant Editor Gillian Bucky
Copy Editor James Guiry
Editorial Assistant Susan DeRosa
Deputy Copy Chief Ellen Scordato
Associate Picture Editor Juliette Dickstein
Picture Researcher Ann Levy
Senior Designer Laurie Jewell
Design Assistant Laura Lang
Production Coordinator Joseph Romano
Cover Illustration Alan J. Nahigian

Library of Congress Cataloging in Publication Data
3 5 7 9 8 6 4 2

Jakoubek, Robert E.
   Adam Clayton Powell, Jr./Robert E. Jakoubek.
      p.   cm.—(Black Americans of achievement)
   Bibliography: p.
   Includes index.
   Summary: Follows the life of the black politician who rose to great power in the House of Representatives during the post–Depression era and became an influential black leader.
   ISBN 1-55546-606-0
        0-7910-0213-6 (pbk.)
   1. Powell, Adam Clayton, 1908–1972—Juvenile literature. 2. Legislators—United States—Biography—Juvenile literature. 3. United States. Congress. House—Biography—Juvenile literature. 4. Afro-Americans—Biography—Juvenile literature. [1. Powell, Adam Clayton, 1908–1972. 2. Legislators. 3. Afro-Americans—Biography] I. Title. II. Series.
E748.P86J35 1988   973'.0496073024—dc19 [B] [92]
87-28739
                              CIP
                              AC

CONTENTS

———— ✿ ————

BLACK
AMERICANS
OF
ACHIEVEMENT

—◈—

MUHAMMAD ALI
heavyweight champion

RICHARD ALLEN
*founder of the
African Methodist
Episcopal church*

LOUIS ARMSTRONG
musician

JAMES BALDWIN
author

BENJAMIN BANNEKER
*scientist and
mathematician*

MARY MCLEOD BETHUNE
educator

BLANCHE K. BRUCE
politician

RALPH BUNCHE
diplomat

GEORGE WASHINGTON CARVER
botanist

CHARLES WADDELL CHESTNUTT
author

PAUL CUFFE
abolitionist

FREDERICK DOUGLASS
abolitionist editor

CHARLES R. DREW
physician

W. E. B. DUBOIS
educator and author

PAUL LAURENCE DUNBAR
poet

DUKE ELLINGTON
bandleader and composer

RALPH ELLISON
author

ELLA FITZGERALD
singer

MARCUS GARVEY
black-nationalist leader

PRINCE HALL
social reformer

WILLIAM H. HASTIE
educator and politician

MATTHEW A. HENSON
explorer

CHESTER HIMES
author

BILLIE HOLIDAY
singer

JOHN HOPE
educator

LENA HORNE
entertainer

LANGSTON HUGHES
poet

JAMES WELDON JOHNSON
author

SCOTT JOPLIN
composer

MARTIN LUTHER KING, JR.
civil rights leader

JOE LOUIS
heavyweight champion

MALCOLM X
militant black leader

THURGOOD MARSHALL
Supreme Court justice

ELIJAH MUHAMMAD
religious leader

JESSE OWENS
champion athlete

GORDON PARKS
photographer

SIDNEY POITIER
actor

ADAM CLAYTON POWELL, JR.
political leader

A. PHILIP RANDOLPH
labor leader

PAUL ROBESON
singer and actor

JACKIE ROBINSON
baseball great

JOHN RUSSWURM
publisher

SOJOURNER TRUTH
antislavery activist

HARRIET TUBMAN
antislavery activist

NAT TURNER
slave revolt leader

DENMARK VESEY
slave revolt leader

MADAME C. J. WALKER
entrepreneur

BOOKER T. WASHINGTON
educator

WALTER WHITE
political activist

RICHARD WRIGHT
author

ON
ACHIEVEMENT

———— •◐• ————

Coretta Scott King

BEFORE YOU BEGIN this book, I hope you will ask yourself what the word excellence means to you. I think that it's a question we should all ask, and keep asking as we grow older and change. Because the truest answer to it should never change. When you think of excellence, perhaps you think of success at work; or of becoming wealthy; or meeting the right person, getting married, and having a good family life.

Those important goals are worth striving for, but there is a better way to look at excellence. As Martin Luther King, Jr., said in one of his last sermons, "I want you to be first in love. I want you to be first in moral excellence. I want you to be first in generosity. If you want to be important, wonderful. If you want to be great, wonderful. But recognize that he who is greatest among you shall be your servant."

My husband, Martin Luther King, Jr., knew that the true meaning of achievement is service. When I met him, in 1952, he was already ordained as a Baptist preacher and was working towards a doctoral degree at Boston University. I was studying at the New England Conservatory and dreamed of accomplishments in music. We married a year later, and after I graduated the following year we moved to Montgomery, Alabama. We didn't know it then, but our notions of achievement were about to undergo a dramatic change.

You may have read or heard about what happened next. What began with the boycott of a local bus line grew into a national movement, and by the time he was assassinated in 1968 my husband had fashioned a black movement powerful enough to shatter forever the practice of racial segregation. What you may not have read about is where he got his method for resisting injustice without compromising his religious beliefs.

He got the strategy of nonviolence from a man of a different race, who lived in a distant country, and even practiced a different religion. The man was Mahatma Gandhi, the great leader of India, who devoted his life to serving humanity in the spirit of love and nonviolence. It was in these principles that Martin discovered his method for social reform. More than anything else, those two principles were the key to his achievements.

This book is about black Americans who served society through the excellence of their achievements. It forms a part of the rich history of black men and women in America—a history of stunning accomplishments in every field of human endeavor, from literature and art to science, industry, education, diplomacy, athletics, jurisprudence, even polar exploration.

Not all of the people in this history had the same ideals, but I think you will find something that all of them have in common. Like Martin Luther King, Jr., they all decided to become "drum majors" and serve humanity. In that principle—whether it was expressed in books, inventions, or song—they found something outside themselves to use as a goal and a guide. Something that showed them a way to serve others, instead of living only for themselves.

Reading the stories of these courageous men and women not only helps us discover the principles that we will use to guide our own lives, but it teaches us about our black heritage and about America itself. It is crucial for us to know the heroes and heroines of our history and to realize that the price we paid in our struggle for equality in America was dear. But we must also understand that we have gotten as far as we have partly because America's democratic system and ideals made it possible.

We still are struggling with racism and prejudice. But the great men and women in this series are a tribute to the spirit of our democratic ideals and the system in which they have flourished. And that makes their stories special, and worth knowing. ✺

ADAM CLAYTON
POWELL, JR.

1

THE BOMB THROWER

A DAM CLAYTON POWELL, Jr., first took his seat as a member of the House of Representatives when the 79th Congress of the United States convened on January 3, 1945. A few days later, the 36-year-old congressman from New York City's Harlem district called on the Speaker of the House, Representative Sam Rayburn of Texas, as a traditional courtesy. As Powell reached out to shake the Democratic leader's hand, he felt both thrilled and nervous, for Rayburn, a veteran of three decades in the House, was the most powerful man in Congress. If a freshman Democratic congressman such as Powell did not earn the Speaker's goodwill, he had little hope of making a mark in the nation's capital.

After Rayburn greeted Powell, he leaned back in his chair, carefully eyed the new congressman, and said, "Adam, everybody down here expects you to come in with a bomb in both hands. Now don't do that, Adam. Oh, I know all about you and I know that you can't be quiet very long but don't throw those bombs. Just see how things operate here. Take your time. Freshmen members of Congress are sup-

Powell was the first U.S. congressman to represent the district of Harlem in New York City. His 25 years of service in the House of Representatives began on January 3, 1945, with the opening session of the 79th Congress.

11

Representative Sam Rayburn, a Democrat from Texas, became the Speaker of the House in 1940 and held the position for nearly 18 years. By the time Powell entered Congress in 1945, Rayburn had already become one of the most influential politicians in the nation's capital.

posed not to be heard and not even to be seen too much. There are a lot of good men around here. Listen to what they have to say, drink it all in, get re-elected a few more times, and then start moving. But for God's sake, Adam, don't throw those bombs."

Powell returned the Speaker's steady gaze and replied, "Mr. Speaker, I've got a bomb in each hand and I'm going to throw them right away."

Powell's comment startled Rayburn. However, a smile soon creased the old man's face, and he began to chuckle. An instant later, both he and Powell were laughing uproariously at Powell's audacity.

Despite Powell's show of good humor, he was often angry and impatient as a congressman. As the minister of the Abyssinian Baptist Church in Harlem (as was his father), he had witnessed the terrible suffering of black Americans during the Great Depression of the 1930s and had discovered within himself the strength and determination to become an effective, militant champion of black equality. When he ran for Congress so he could serve the people of Harlem in ways that he could not as a minister, he received an overwhelming number of votes.

Yet the brash young congressman was met by a wall of demeaning, discriminatory rules when he first arrived in Washington, D.C. Not a single hotel near the Capitol would rent him a room. Lunch counters would not serve him a cup of coffee. Downtown theaters would not even let him sit in their balconies: Shortly after his arrival, Powell and Hazel Scott, his fiancée, went to see *Rhapsody in Blue*, the film biography of the composer George Gershwin. Scott had a starring part in the film. When the couple tried to enter the theater, the manager stopped them at the door, unwilling to admit them because they were black.

Powell discovered that racial barriers stood just as high on Capitol Hill. He was told, discreetly, that certain facilities in the congressional quarters were

off limits: the dining room, the gymnasium, the steam baths, the barbershop, the swimming pool. Yet he would not be stopped. He soon barged into these restricted facilities even though he did not want to swim or work out or receive a haircut.

Powell insisted to his staff that they follow his example. "When I heard that the dining room for Representatives' staff was off limits to Negroes," he said, "I told my secretary and clerks to go down there and eat whether they were hungry or not!" His confrontational tactics won him few friends among his white colleagues, but they earned him the grudging respect of even his bitterest opponents.

Jazz pianist and singer Hazel Scott became Powell's wife shortly after he arrived in Washington, D.C., to begin his first term as a congressman. She is shown here in a scene from one of her films, Rhapsody in Blue.

Powell in his Washington, D.C., office after completing his first week as a congressman in 1945. He and William Dawson, a Democrat from Illinois, were then the only two blacks in Congress.

Powell eventually rose to a position of great influence and power in Congress, steadfastly refusing to play any games of deference and courtesy with other congressmen. A close friend who remembered his often irritating ways said: "I can see why white people hated Adam. Boy, Adam would really strut. We'd be walking down the corridor and we would pass a big chairman of some committee and Adam wouldn't speak to him, just keep walking, talking to me or somebody else. Then he'd go down in the elevator and enter the subway and start to kid with the guys on the subway. To the cleaning woman he'd say, 'Hello, baby; hello, baby'; to the congressman he wouldn't open his mouth.''

For a decade, Powell was one of only two blacks to serve as a congressman. Consequently, the desks in his office overflowed with letters containing requests from blacks who lived far from his congressional district. "Millions of Negro people in the South had no congressman to speak for them," he maintained. "They were the disenfranchised, the ostracized, the exploited, and when they pressed upon me their many problems of many years, I could not refuse them because I love all people."

And they loved him. Even during Powell's last years, when his fortunes had greatly declined, people would still come up to him and tell him how much he had meant to them—how they had cheered as he hurled his bombs at the bastions of racial discrimination—and how they had rejoiced as the racial barriers came tumbling down. ❧

2

FATHER
AND
SON

❧

ADAM CLAYTON POWELL, Jr., was born in New Haven, Connecticut, on November 29, 1908, shortly before his family moved to Harlem. Many years later, when Congress was in recess, he enjoyed driving a fancy powder-blue Jaguar around Harlem. However, he made a point of never driving along 134th Street between Seventh and Eighth avenues. The neighborhood had become an unpleasant slum, and it pained him to see what had once been a quiet and refined block reduced to such squalor. It had been on this street—a few blocks from the wealthy black neighborhood known as Striver's Row—that he had grown up.

Adam's family had owned a spacious brownstone with a tree-shaded backyard on West 134th Street. The house had a sitting room for his mother, a study reserved for his father, and a parlor that was rarely used. There were a maid and two housekeepers who served breakfasts of muffins, biscuits, and pancakes and dinners that began with fresh oysters on a table set with fine crystal and china and linen napkins in silver rings.

Life had not always been so kind to the Powells.

Boasting the largest and wealthiest black Baptist congregation in America, the Abyssinian Baptist Church moved to Harlem from midtown New York in 1923. Throughout Powell's childhood, his father was the head of this influential spiritual center.

In the years before the senior Powell became a successful minister, his life was filled with hardship. While he was growing up in Virginia, he and his family lived in a small cabin much like the one shown here.

The patriarch of the household, Adam Clayton Powell, Sr., was born in rural Virginia in 1865, the year that the Civil War ended. He was light skinned and of mixed black, white, and Cherokee Indian ancestry. His father's identity was not known to him, but his mother was Sally Dunnings, whose family owned a small farm. The Dunningses were free blacks—a tiny minority of southern blacks who had been free prior to the end of slavery. In 1867, Sally Dunnings married Anthony Powell, a former slave from a nearby plantation. It was from his stepfather that Adam Powell, Sr., received his last name.

Times were hard in the South in the years after the Civil War, largely because the region's agriculture had been ruined in the fighting. In 1870, the Dun-

ningses were forced to sell their farm. Five-year-old
Adam Powell, his mother and stepfather, and six
other members of the Dunning family then began to
work on a local tobacco farm as sharecroppers, tilling
a plot of ground and giving most of what they raised
to the landowner. The elder Powell's earliest mem-
ories were of miserable poverty. His large family lived
together in a cramped one-room cabin and rose before
dawn each morning to farm five acres of land. When
the crops failed during one year, the family was forced
to live on dried apples and black-eyed peas for six
weeks.

When the elder Powell was 10 years old, his family
moved to West Virginia, hoping for a better life.
Adam, Jr.'s, father lived there for eight years and
grew to young adulthood. However, it was a time,
he said, "of mental and moral disaster." All he wanted
was "a pistol, a pair of brass knuckles and a jug of
hard liquor." When he was 19 years old, he got into
extreme trouble and had to leave his home under the
cover of darkness. He soon found work as a coal miner
in Ohio, but his $100-a-month wage was quickly
spent during constant nights of gambling and ca-
rousing.

One Sunday morning after a particularly wild Saturday night, the elder Powell sat on the side of his
bed and looked at his reflection in a broken mirror.
As he stared at himself, he felt that he was struck by
a divine command to mend his ways. That same day,
he entered the town's Baptist church, walked down
the center aisle, joined the congregation, and was
baptized. Within two months, he had saved enough
money to pay off his debts. He began to teach Sunday
school and was soon enrolled in a seminary. He was
studying to become a minister.

After finishing his theological studies, Adam's
father searched for a congregation. In September 1893,
he became the pastor of an impoverished black church
in New Haven, Connecticut. During the next 15

While the minister of Abyssinia, the Reverend Adam Clayton Powell, Sr., also became wealthy from a number of successful ventures in the Harlem real estate market. Such dealings enabled his son to grow up in an affluent household.

years, he built the church into a widely respected institution and, in the process, gathered considerable acclaim.

Shortly before the Reverend Adam Powell moved to New Haven, he married Mattie Fletcher Shaefer, his childhood sweetheart, from West Virginia. In 1898, she gave birth to a daughter, Blanche. Ten years later, on Thanksgiving Day, a son arrived and was named Adam Clayton Powell, Jr.

By the time Adam was born, his father had grown restless, maintaining that "I was too full of energy to remain long in New Haven. I needed a heavy load to steady me." The reverend's heavy load was given to him in late 1908, when the Abyssinian Baptist Church in New York City asked him to become its minister. One of the oldest churches in the city, Abyssinia (as it was also called) bore the ancient name for Ethiopia and was a symbol of black Americans' interest in their African heritage. Located in the western area of New York's midtown, the church had just celebrated its centennial. Yet it faced many problems. Adam, Jr., said that when his father came to Abyssinia, it offered little more than "age, and old time Negro aristocracy, and debts." Worse, the church stood in the middle of New York's red-light district, and the new minister watched in horror while prostitutes solicited men as they left his Sunday service.

The Reverend Adam Powell revitalized the church, greatly increasing its membership and restoring it to a sound financial position. Working with local reformers, he helped to clean up the neighborhood. He joined with former president Theodore Roosevelt in organizing the Anti-Saloon League and cried out against the dangers of whiskey drinking. The reverend also launched a campaign against the brothels in the area, and he became the target of much abuse from the local prostitutes. On one occasion when young Adam was walking on a street beside his father, his suit was spattered by refuse thrown from the roof of a brothel.

The key to the Reverend Adam Powell's success in his church and in the community lay in his eloquence in the pulpit. "He was awesome," his son said, "as he thundered his holy invectives against the sins of the day. He preached so hard that his starched collar and cuffs were always wilted." The reverend forever impressed young Kenneth Clark, who later became a prominent sociologist. Clark said, "When, as a child, I first saw him, I thought he was God."

The reverend preached that religion should not merely prepare the faithful for heaven but "ready them to live." He insisted that his church meet "the real needs of the people in the community." At its

The Reverend Adam Clayton Powell, Sr., poses outside Abyssinia with a group of students from his Sunday school. Perhaps the best-known clergyman in Harlem's history, the senior Powell was also one of the most popular.

location on West 40th Street, Abyssinia was in the center of what was then still the most important black section of New York, and he opened the church's doors to its residents. In came the poor for food and financial help, the young for recreation, and large, enthusiastic audiences for music and theater. Yet the Reverend Adam Powell's greatest ambition was to move the church itself. From the moment of his arrival in New York, his eyes had been fixed on a sprawling residential neighborhood just north of Central Park: Harlem, where his dealings in local real estate made him quite wealthy.

The reverend had settled his family in Harlem when he came to New York from New Haven. With newly born Adam in his mother's arms, the Powells had moved into a brownstone on West 134th Street, where the household's life revolved around the reverend's ministry. To fit his schedule and tastes, the family had only two meals a day: a huge breakfast, which always included salted mackerel, and a dinner of several courses that was served at 4:00 P.M.

Throughout Adam's childhood, he was pampered by his family. After breakfast, his father would take him on his lap and read to him from the Bible. He was given a gray Persian lamb coat and patent leather shoes. His mother and sister dressed him in lace-trimmed, page-boy suits and fixed his hair in long curls to give him an appearance similar to that of a popular storybook character, Little Lord Fauntleroy.

When Adam was six years old, he came down with a lung infection that required constant care. Long after his condition improved, his mother sheltered him and kept him away from neighborhood children. Instead, she showered him with pets and toys and sat with him almost every day in a nearby park, while other youngsters roughhoused and played close by. Very early in his life, Adam grew used to being spoiled by women.

Adam gradually emerged from his mother's shadow, and as he did, he learned some of life's lessons. The most painful of the lessons involved his racial identity. While he was growing up, racial relations were often tense in Harlem. One evening when Adam was nine years old, his father sent him out to buy an evening paper. On his way to the newsstand, he was confronted by a group of black youngsters who demanded to know to what race he belonged. Adam had never thought about his light skin color before. He recalled, "I looked at my skin and said, 'White!' Whereupon I was promptly and thoroughly beaten." The next night, his mother sent him on an errand, and he was accosted by a gang of white youths, who also asked him about his skin color. "Remembering my answer, and my beating of the preceding night, I answered 'Colored!' Whereupon I was again bloodied." The episode was his first brush with racism.

Adam's uncertainty about his racial identity was understandable. The Powells were fair skinned and had straight hair. In the phrase of the day, they could have "passed for white." While preaching at Abyssinia, his father asserted his pride in being black and championed racial justice. But at home, Adam recalled, "there was never any consciousness of race," and his parents did not mention the family's black heritage.

The question of race was not the only matter that Adam found puzzling. His father required that all the members of the Powell household lead upstanding lives as an example for other members of the community. But old habits die hard. When Adam was a youngster, he found some empty gin bottles in his father's drawer. When he asked his father about them, the reverend stated that although he often gave sermons cautioning against the use of whiskey, he had never said a bad word about gin. Such conflicting messages were confusing to Adam, and he grew up

The Powell family moved to Harlem in 1908, shortly after Adam, Jr.'s birth. Originally a white community, Harlem was then becoming the most heavily populated area for blacks in America.

holding somewhat more lax moral standards than those preached by his father in church. In addition, being in the shadow of such a dominating father eventually fostered a deeply competitive drive within Adam, so he did not always act as his father had asked.

Adam ultimately discovered the black world on the streets of Harlem. During his youth, Harlem became the largest and most fabled black community in the United States. A collapsed real estate boom after the turn of the century had opened up street after street of brownstone houses at bargain prices. Caught in a "Harlem fever," blacks left the crowded slums in lower Manhattan and moved north. They were joined by thousands more from the rural South and from the West Indies. By 1920, 73,000 blacks lived above 110th Street, the district's lower boundary; the black population in Harlem would swell to more than 160,000 by 1930. During this period of growth, the district became the center of a tremendous development in black music, literature, art, and theater that became known as the Harlem Renaissance.

Harlem assumed a great political distinction when Marcus Garvey, a Jamaican immigrant, arrived in the district in 1916 and soon after organized the Universal Negro Improvement Association, the first mass movement of blacks in American history. He appealed to black pride, denounced integration and promoted black separatism, and envisioned the day when black Americans would return to Africa and free the continent from the bonds of its European colonial masters. In flamboyant, colorful uniforms, Garvey and his followers staged parades through Harlem's streets. Adam took it all in with wide-eyed awe. "One of the greatest thrills of my life, when I was about ten or twelve years old," he said, "was to sit at Garvey's feet, or roll down Seventh Avenue with him as he paraded in his white plumed hat."

When Powell was seven years old, black-nationalist leader Marcus Garvey (shown here) came to Harlem and established the Universal Negro Improvement Association in an attempt to promote black separatism. Powell greatly admired Garvey's appeals to racial pride.

Garveyism was eventually destroyed after the organization engaged in misguided business ventures and its founder was imprisoned after being found guilty on a questionable charge of mail fraud. Nevertheless, Garvey left a deep impression on Adam and millions of other blacks. Adam later wrote that Garvey "brought to the Negro people for the first time a sense of pride in being black."

The Reverend Adam Powell had long seen the promise of Harlem. As early as 1911, he had decided that it was Abyssinia's "final destination." However, it was no easy matter for a church as large as his to pick up and move. Years of planning and fund-raising nearly exhausted the congregation. Yet the great day finally came: On February 25, 1923, the reverend celebrated the first service in the vast, new Abyssi-

A photograph of Powell from the Townsend Harris High School Yearbook, which listed basketball, football, and track among his extracurricular activities.

nian Baptist Church at 138th Street and Lenox Avenue—the very heart of Harlem. He expressed his hope during the inaugural ceremony that the new church would be a "social welfare center for colored people" and "help save them physically, mentally and morally." As the Reverend had hoped, Abyssinia thrived in its new location. Its congregation soon grew to more than 10,000 members—the largest of any Protestant church in America.

When Adam was 12 years old, he stood 6 feet tall but weighed only 100 pounds. Because of his height, he had a natural advantage at basketball and spent hour after hour practicing and playing the game. An avid reader, he was a good student in elementary school and was far ahead of his classmates. But his grades suffered once he entered Townsend Harris High School, a college preparatory school that he attended when he was a teenager. During this period—the early 1920s—he began spending more time socializing with his friends than studying. He also paid a lot of attention to girls. "He didn't chase them any harder than they chased him," a friend recalled. "The girls just loved him."

Adam graduated from high school in January 1925 with no definite plans about his future. However, his father insisted that Adam go to college, so in September 1925, prodded by the reverend, he enrolled at the City College of New York. It was an unsuccessful venture. He recalled, "I began using the time that should have been devoted to my college work for the extracurricular—having a good time, going to parties, drinking, smoking, being spoiled by women in new ways—so that at the end of the first semester I failed three subjects."

During the next term, Adam failed every course and flunked out of school. The "extracurricular" was not the sole reason for his poor scholarship. In March 1926, his sister, Blanche—"my real love, my pas-

In 1925, Powell began his studies at the City College of New York. He left the school one year later, after having failed most of his courses. He then entered Colgate University in upstate New York and lived away from Harlem for the first time in his life.

sionate love"—died after an operation. Adam was devastated.

Perhaps understanding his son's grief, the Reverend Adam Powell offered him a second chance at a college education and arranged for his admission to Colgate University in rural upstate New York, far from the temptations of the big city. For a young man from Harlem, Colgate sometimes seemed to be a million miles away from home. He tried to fit into the virtually all-white student body by keeping quiet about racial issues, neither identifying with the handful of blacks on campus nor saying anything to white students about his being black. But in the spring of 1927, an all-white fraternity to which he was pledged looked into his background and rejected him. A short while later, his father came to Colgate and gave a lecture in the school's chapel about racial tolerance. Adam returned to his dormitory room and found a note from his roommate: "I can't live with you anymore because of the way your father defended Negroes today—you must be a Negro!" Colgate sided with the roommate

Powell was deeply affected by the death of his older sister, Blanche, in 1926. In this illustration, her image has been superimposed over a photograph of her funeral at Abyssinia.

and forced Adam to move to another dormitory. After this incident, Adam identified more closely with Colgate's blacks and pledged to a black fraternity.

Still, in these years, he was often taken for white. One summer he had a job as a bellhop at the exclusive Equinox Hotel in Vermont, near the home of Robert Todd Lincoln, the aged son of Abraham Lincoln. A regular at the hotel's dining room, Lincoln's son would sweep up to the Equinox's front entrance nearly every evening in his shiny Rolls-Royce. The bellhops—all of whom were black—had to race to the car each night and open the door. And each night, a young black man was subjected to a painful humiliation: The bigoted Lincoln, seeing a black bellhop's hand on the chrome of his car door, would raise his cane and strike the bellhop across the knuckles. Because of Lincoln's behavior, the hotel's manager asked Adam if he would intervene. According to Adam, "I, whose father had been raised by a branded slave, would open his door. And Mr. Lincoln, looking at my white hand, was satisfied." He would smile and tip Adam a dollar each night.

Adam did not abandon his fun-loving ways at Colgate. He was frequently out until late in the night partying with friends and going on wild rides on country roads. When he finally learned to separate business from pleasure, he started to attend class regularly, studied hard in the library, and received reasonably good grades.

On June 9, 1930, Adam graduated from Colgate, and his proud parents presented him with a two-month tour of Europe and the Middle East. With $2,500 in his pocket, he sailed on the maiden voyage of the German liner *Bremen*. A new yet familiar career would be awaiting him when he returned home. ❧

3

A FLAMING TONGUE

W HEN POWELL WAS a child, he frequently stood in the pulpit next to his father during Sunday services. Many in the congregation at Abyssinia took it for granted that the youngster would follow in his father's footsteps. But Powell seemed indifferent to the ministry, and his father knew better than to pressure him. Years later, the younger Powell recalled that in his youth his parents "never advised me or encouraged me in the slightest to go into the ministry." At Colgate, he had initially studied courses that would prepare him for a career as a physician, and he aimed to be admitted to the Harvard Medical School.

Medicine was a fine, honorable profession, but the elder Powell wanted his son to be a minister. Early in Powell's years at Colgate, the reverend had approached his son's closest friend in college, Ray Vaughan, asking him to persuade the younger Powell to change his major from premed to theology. A few days later, as the two young men were driving a Model A Ford back to school after a weekend in New York City, Vaughan raised the subject of the ministry. To his amazement, Powell needed no convincing. As they jolted along the rough roads of upstate New York, Powell agreed that succeeding his father was too good a chance to pass up. "He realized that it was all set up for him," Vaughan said. "All he had to do was walk in and take over."

In 1930, Powell was appointed the assistant minister and business manager of Abyssinia. He made use of his influential post by becoming active in various social and political issues.

Isabel Washington first met Powell in 1929, while she was performing at the prestigious Cotton Club in Harlem. They were married by Powell's father nearly four years later at Abyssinia.

Powell's parents were overjoyed at their son's decision. When he called and told them about his choice, he said, "the tears of happiness flowed over the phone." The position of assistant minister and business manager of the Abyssinian Baptist Church awaited him at the conclusion of his European holiday.

When Powell returned from his trip to Europe and the Middle East in September 1930, he was met at the pier by his father's expensive Pierce Arrow limousine. As he rode back home to Harlem, he mav have noticed some changes in the city. He may well have seen more than the usual number of boarded-up storefronts, or sad-faced men selling apples on street corners, or a long line of people waiting patiently in front of a soup kitchen for a free meal. With each passing day, the United States was falling deeper and deeper into the worst economic calamity in its history, the Great Depression.

On the other hand, Powell may not have paid the signs of hard times any notice at all. He had something else on his mind. He was in love.

During Powell's later years at Colgate, he had frequently traveled to New York City to take advantage of its nightlife. Because of his light-colored skin, he was one of the few blacks who could enter the Cotton Club and Harlem's other exclusive nightclubs where only whites were admitted. In these clubs, audiences were entertained by black performers such as Ethel Waters, Bill "Bojangles" Robinson, and Duke Ellington and His Orchestra. Powell was popular with many of the clubs' show girls. In fact, when he gave his first trial sermon at Abyssinia, on Good Friday in 1929, more than one of the ladies from the Cotton Club was in the congregation.

Two days after that sermon, Powell met a singer and actress named Isabel Washington, who was a star at the Cotton Club, and their romance blossomed. He came to New York to visit her on weekends, and she often traveled to Colgate to see him.

When Powell brought Isabel home for the first time, his father barely spoke to her. The reverend believed that she was thoroughly unsuitable for a man who was destined for the pulpit. She would shock Abyssinia's congregation with her background as a blues singer. Consequently, he strongly disapproved of the match and did everything he could to break up the couple. One of the reasons why he gave his son a transatlantic trip after he finished college was to get him away from Isabel. Yet Powell came back more in love with Isabel than when he had left.

After returning from his trip, Powell prepared himself for the ministry by enrolling at the distinguished Union Theological Seminary in New York in the fall of 1930. However, he had a falling-out with the seminary's director before long and withdrew from the school. He then entered the Teachers College of Columbia University. He would later say that most of his progressive thinking on religious and social questions had been formed by his Columbia professors. In 1932, he graduated with a master's degree in religious studies.

In March of the following year, the reverend finally gave his blessing to his son and Isabel and presided over their marriage in a ceremony at Abyssinia. Powell's father still had grave reservations about the marriage, yet in the two and a half years since returning from Europe, his son had more than proven himself. Powell had thrown himself completely into the work of the church and into the life of Harlem. "My father said he built the church and I would interpret it. This I made up my mind to do," he said. "I intended to fashion that church into a mighty weapon, keen-edged and sharp-pointed." Although Powell was able to argue the fine points of biblical and theological questions with the most learned of scholars, his real interest at Abyssinia lay in social activism. He wanted the church and its pastors to fight for Harlem and its residents.

When Powell returned to Harlem in 1930, he began to observe the effects of the Great Depression on life in the black community. By the middle of the decade, nearly one out of every five blacks in Harlem was unemployed. Shown here is 125th Street, the district's main thoroughfare.

Whatever progress blacks had made in American society during the prosperous 1920s was undone by the Great Depression. Between 1929 and 1932, the median income of black families in Harlem fell by almost half. In the neighborhood of the Abyssinian Baptist Church, nearly two-thirds of the schoolchildren went undernourished. Black workers who had a job were very fortunate. Approximately 40,000 Harlem blacks were out of work by the end of 1931. Racism made matters even more intolerable. The old adage that blacks were the "last hired and first fired" was never truer. The human suffering during these hard times was immeasurable.

One stormy day during the early stages of the Great Depression, Powell and a friend were driving around the city. Suddenly, they came across hundreds of rain-drenched black women standing beside a brick wall. Powell pulled to a stop. Puzzled, he asked his companion why the women were standing there. She told him that the women were maids, laundresses, and other unemployed domestic workers who stood outside throughout the day and much of the night waiting for someone to hire them to work for 10 cents an hour.

In the first years of the depression, during the Republican administration of President Herbert Hoover, the federal government did not assume any responsibility for aiding the unemployed. The burden of extending a helping hand to the desperate was left to local governments and private charities. Surrounded on all sides by human suffering, Abyssinia did what it could. The Reverend Adam Powell organized an extensive relief effort and placed his new assistant minister—a 22-year-old, fresh out of college—in charge. Powell supervised a free food program and saw to it that the church's community house gave shelter to the homeless. Working with the church's staff, he collected used clothing and distributed it to the poor. In the first four months of this program, the church served nearly 29,000 free meals and gave away thousands of garments.

Powell also gave of himself. A church worker remembered the time a poor man came in on a bitter winter day: "I called upstairs, 'Adam, I have a man down here that has no shoes on. And it's cold!' He called back, 'You're telling me—I've only got two pairs myself.' But he said, 'Wait a minute,' and he sent down one of his pairs of shoes for the man. Anytime I needed anything for a big man I'd call Adam and he would share his things."

However, there was a limit to how much money the better-off members of the church could contribute. Consequently, the relief program had to be cut back during 1931 and 1932. As the depression deepened, nearly every charity in the United States faced the same problem. Only in 1933, under the administration of a new president, Franklin Delano Roosevelt, did the federal government begin providing direct relief to the unemployed. Roosevelt also in-

Food is distributed to a group of hungry Harlem children during the Great Depression. In the early 1930s, Powell was the head of a relief program that gave out food and clothing to the needy.

stituted a series of programs, which he called the "New Deal," to restore the nation's economy.

One evening in early 1933, five Harlem doctors called at Powell's apartment in the church. The physicians said they needed him to be "a flaming tongue, to fight our battle." The five men explained that they had been barred from practicing at Harlem Hospital, the community's only public health institution. They had been barred for one reason: They were black. The hospital had a bad reputation in Harlem; some called it "the Butcher Shop" because of the horrible care that patients received there. After suffering through years of inferior medical service and years of segregating most of the black hospital employees into menial jobs, the firing of the five doctors came as the crowning blow to the black community.

Powell helped to form a committee to deal with Harlem Hospital. He staged a mass meeting and led a picket line, but reforms did not come quickly. The hospital's superintendent refused to see him. When Powell took his complaints to John O'Brien, the mayor of New York, O'Brien put a hand on his shoulder and said, "Go back to Harlem, boy, and don't fan the flames."

Powell did just the opposite. In April 1933, he called for a demonstration on the steps of City Hall. He hoped that a few hundred supporters would show up. Instead, several thousand people traveled downtown from Harlem, packing the subways and buses. "I had to stand on a bench and finally on top of a car in order to talk to them," Powell said. "These were six thousand people marching together; they were my people, and I belonged to them." Deciding to put on a dramatic demonstration, he charged up the steps of City Hall, went inside, and put his case against the hospital to the Board of Estimate, the city's highest legislative body. He wrote of his feelings after the demonstration: "All my life I had been preparing for this moment and yet had never been conscious of it."

Powell had grabbed the spotlight, and to some extent his leadership was successful. The Board of Estimate agreed to investigate conditions at the hospital, and over the next few years the situation slowly improved. Yet other activists had actually done the hard, day-to-day organizational work even though Powell received most of the credit for the demonstration. In the midst of the protest, he had left for a lengthy honeymoon with Isabel, returning just in time for the dramatics at City Hall. Leading a crowd was something he could not miss.

On March 19, 1935, Harlem exploded into a serious riot. At 4:00 that afternoon, a 16-year-old boy was caught stealing a penknife in a dime store on 125th Street, Harlem's main shopping avenue. A store detective hustled the boy into a back room and threatened him with a beating. Customers left the store excitedly, telling the news that a black youth

When white-owned shops in Harlem were looted by rioters in 1935, Powell quickly organized a committee to combat the racial discrimination and despair that had led to the violence.

was about to be beaten. Rumors spread through the community. A crowd, furious at the store's white owners, gathered on the sidewalk. One bottle after another was thrown by people in the crowd, and the store's plate glass windows shattered. The violence soon spread. Stores and businesses were broken into and looted. Rioting gripped Harlem and lasted throughout the night. The next morning, 125th Street looked like a war zone. One man lay dead and 200 were injured while more than 300 establishments had been looted.

The riots stunned the city even though trouble had been brewing for a long while. The discriminatory practices of the merchants along 125th Street had especially embittered the neighborhood. Although the shoppers were black, nearly all of the stores were owned by whites who either refused to employ blacks or would hire them for only the most menial tasks. Harlemites called the street "The Great White Way." Powell recognized the depth of their anger at never seeing a black salesperson and warned that violence would soon occur again unless the unfair policies of the Harlem businesses came to an end.

The morning after the riot, Powell held a meeting in his apartment and organized the Emergency Citizens Committee, a group that demanded an end to discrimination. However, political divisions among its members made concerted action difficult, and the organization soon fell apart.

Three years passed before Powell was able to organize a successful pressure group. On February 12, 1938, 2,000 people crowded into the Abyssinian Baptist Church and heard him proclaim the formation of the Greater New York Coordinating Committee on Employment. The new organization aimed to use persuasion, pickets, and boycotts against employers who discriminated against blacks.

Adam Clayton Powell, Sr., was the pastor of Abyssinia for nearly 30 years. He finally gave up the post in 1937, when his son threatened to leave the church if he was not made the minister.

The committee members first targeted the Consolidated Edison Company, New York's gas and electric utility. They picketed the company's offices and warned that unless the utility started hiring blacks, Harlemites would stop using electricity for one day of every week in order to disrupt the company's service. Next, the committee attacked the New York Bell Telephone Company, not one of whose 4,500 operators was black. The committee promised that unless the company changed its hiring practices, blacks in Harlem would tie up the system by dialing for operator assistance again and again. Both companies wanted to avoid chaos, and they quickly negotiated agreements with the committee. However, the agreements were full of loopholes, and few blacks were given jobs.

The white-owned businesses along 125th Street continued to upset Harlem's residents, and the committee stepped up its campaign for black employment. "We began to picket 125th Street stores from river to river," Powell said. "We made it a disgrace for anyone in Harlem to cross a picket line." Using the slogan Don't Buy Where You Can't Work, the committee inflicted serious economic losses on the merchants. Grudgingly, the store owners gave in to some of the demands and promised that in the future at least one-third of their salespeople would be black.

Under Powell's leadership, the committee also won concessions from bakeries and bottling companies. The New York World's Fair of 1939 had a whites-only employment policy until committee picketers showed up at the fairgrounds. Soon after, the fair's organizers started hiring blacks. Powell was even more successful leading the committee against the city's bus lines. Using boycotts and pickets against both the bus companies and the bus drivers' union, the committee won places behind the wheel for blacks. Until then, all bus drivers in New York had been white.

Powell was soon a commanding figure in Harlem, eclipsing even his father. Although he was still only the assistant minister at Abyssinia, he preached more than half the Sunday sermons. He felt ready to take command and told his father in 1937 that he "wanted to be top man." Although 72 years old and not in the best of health, the elder Powell resisted. But when his 28-year-old son said he would leave Abyssinia if he could not be pastor, the old man accepted the inevitable. In September 1937, the Reverend Adam Powell resigned, and the church's deacons and trustees unanimously elected his son to be his successor.

On November 21, 1937, Powell became Abyssinia's pastor. In a fashionably cut dark coat and gray pinstriped trousers, he presented a striking figure. More than 3,000 worshipers—many of them white, many of them from distant cities—filled the pews to celebrate his swift rise to fame and influence. *Life* magazine covered the event and hailed it as a star-studded gala. Another magazine described Powell as the "outstanding liberal among younger men in the ministry." The congregation sat silently as the senior Powell, now the pastor emeritus, rose to the pulpit and turned to his son: "You got a message, my son, not from the schools you have attended, not from the books you have read; you got a message from the Holy Ghost: Deliver it though people shoot at you." ✢

Powell said that as a clergyman he "intended to move the people out of the church where God was—along the avenues and byways where hundreds of thousands were languishing in hopeless squalor."

4

THE RISING
POLITICIAN

EARLY IN 1941, Powell visited the New York
office of Wendell Willkie, a businessman who the
year before had astounded nearly everyone by win-
ning the Republican nomination for president. A
political novice—he had never held any public office—Willkie lost the election to President Roosevelt, but his vibrant personality and unconventional
independence made an impression on many Americans, including Powell.

Almost alone among political leaders of the day,
Willkie spoke out for racial equality. He had plans
for future campaigns and wanted the support of black
voters, and he reasoned that the young minister from
Harlem might be a bridge to their support. Powell
went to visit him, and the two men talked for a long
time. At last, Willkie looked intently at his visitor
and said, "I would like you to be part of my team. I
would like you to play a major role. I like indepen-
dents. But whether you join my team or not, Powell,
remember this, always keep yourself independent. Don't
let any of the political parties control you."

While driving home, Powell thought about what
Willkie had said. His invitation to Powell was flat-
tering but not really tempting. New York usually voted
overwhelmingly Democratic; siding with a Republi-

*Powell takes his seat as a New York City councilman in January
1942 after being elected by an overwhelming majority.*

43

In 1940, all eyes were upon Republican presidential candidate Wendell Willkie as he battled the incumbent president, Franklin Roosevelt, for the nation's highest office. Willkie encouraged Powell to seek public office.

can would be political suicide for Powell, who had started to think about running for local office.

For decades, organizations such as the National Association for the Advancement of Colored People (NAACP) and the National Urban League had been striving to bring together blacks and liberal whites in support of a strong civil rights movement. Powell hoped to unite New York's black community behind a banner of racial solidarity, and blacks were ready for a strong, charismatic leader like Powell. Even though they formed a powerful voting block, their needs had been largely ignored by city hall, partly because the leading black politicians were dependents of New York's white-controlled political party organizations.

In the early 1940s, New York adopted a new charter that changed the boundaries of its electoral districts. Under the new plan, the district of Harlem was assured a seat on the city council. Willkie's encouragement of Powell's political ambitions convinced the dynamic, 32-year-old minister that he should run for office. He decided to see if he could become New York's first black city councilman in more than two decades.

Although it was Powell's first time standing for office, he was no stranger to politics. His leadership of the Greater New York Coordinating Committee placed him at the center of numerous local issues, from those involving discrimination by bus companies and utilities to the mistreatment of blacks by the management of the World's Fair. Nor were his political views unknown to Harlem voters. Beginning in 1936, he wrote a widely read column, "The Soap Box," for the *Amsterdam News*, New York's premier black newspaper. The column was named for the makeshift platforms that street-corner orators stood on when pleading their causes to crowds that would gather around them on the sidewalks.

In his newspaper column, Powell spoke his mind on a great array of subjects. He wrote about everything from hot weather to sports to dishonest merchants to the rise of fascist dictators such as Adolf Hitler in Germany and Benito Mussolini in Italy. But most of all, he called for blacks to unite and battle racial repression. He deplored the divisions in Harlem—the suspicions between black Americans and recent immigrants from the Caribbean, between light- and dark-skinned blacks, between the poor and the middle class. "Away with a caste system within this race of ours," he cried. "Away with those who feel they are better. . . . The Negro in the valley is hungry and despised, humiliated, oppressed and he's ready to march."

To lead the march for racial equality, Powell turned to the strongest institution in the black community: the church. He expected it to be an "instrument, keen and rugged, fighting exploitation and raising the standards of our race along the entire battle front of human liberties. Upon this basis only does the church deserve to survive."

So intent was Powell on building a strong movement for the advancement of black causes that he even flirted with communism. In the dark days of the depression, the Communist party was particularly active in Harlem. It had gained a following by calling for an end to the exploitation of workers by capitalist businessmen. Some party members sincerely believed in racial equality and took part in protesting racism. But the Communists had only a weak commitment to black progress. The real purpose of American communism was to serve Russian communism, and the party's leaders in the United States had to follow the often contradictory policies that came out of Moscow.

Powell never joined the Communist party, but he did work with its members. He welcomed the Communists' forceful participation in the campaign against Harlem Hospital and in the activities of the Greater New York Coordinating Committee on Employment. But the brutal actions of Soviet leader

A parade of Communist party members winds its way through the streets of Harlem. Because the Communist party was one of the few organizations in the 1930s and 1940s that sought to address the grievances of blacks, Powell often applauded their efforts.

Joseph Stalin, who conducted purges of his political opponents and of millions of helpless peasants, eventually made Powell lose interest in communism.

In any case, Powell would not have made a good member of the Communist party. He was far too independent and free spirited to submit to the discipline required of Communists, or, for that matter, the loyalty asked of staunch Democrats and Republicans.

Political leaders dislike mavericks, and the party bosses of New York had no use for Powell. They ignored him when they were selecting candidates for Harlem's new city council seat in 1941. Instead, both the Democrats and Republicans chose black candidates who were reliable members of their party.

The members of the political clubhouses may have preferred candidates who obeyed the party leadership, but the voters of Harlem did not. When Powell expressed his interest in running as an independent, he got an enthusiastic public response. On Sunday morning, September 23, 1941, he announced from the pulpit at Abyssinia his intention to run. One observer said, "The congregation suddenly turned the sacred meeting into a bedlam of hallelujahs and vociferous handclapping, lasting twenty minutes."

Powell may have been an independent, but he did not lack an effective organization. Abyssinia's huge congregation gave him a priceless base of support. The Greater New York Coordinating Committee on Employment reorganized itself into the People's Committee and worked tirelessly on his behalf. Most importantly, he was a great campaigner. With his good looks and riveting voice, he enraptured street-corner crowds. "I am not seeking a political job," he would say. "I am fighting for the chance to give my people the best representation in the affairs of their city, to help make Harlem the number one community of New York."

Powell is sworn in as a member of the New York City Council. In his first campaign for political office, he received the third-highest vote total among 29 candidates—an amount that was high enough to merit election to the post.

On election day, nearly 90 percent of Harlem's eligible voters turned out and voted for Powell in overwhelming numbers. With Isabel and his proud father looking on, he took the oath of office and assumed a place on the city council on January 1, 1942.

Several of the newspaper photographs of the swearing-in ceremony captured Isabel looking sad and forlorn, with an expression inappropriate for a day of triumph. All was not well with the Powells. After his election, Isabel had turned to her husband and said, "Darling, I know I am going to lose you." Actually, Powell had wandered away years before.

The concern that Isabel would be an improper minister's wife had proved to be groundless. After their marriage in 1933, she completely dropped her acting and singing career. It was no easy decision; she had just been offered the lead role in *Showboat*, one of the greatest Broadway musicals of the 1930s.

Instead, she threw herself into her duties at Abyssinia, standing loyally at her husband's side, entertaining thousands of women, working long hours for church charities. Powell appreciated her devotion, but before long he was seen going into a fashionable nightclub far from Harlem with a handsome woman on his arm while his wife remained at home. "She loved me completely and utterly," he would say later, "yet I grew and she stood still. And as I grew there was absolutely no understanding between us." He left her in 1944, and they were divorced a year later.

The new councilman made his voice heard in city government at a time when world events were having a strong impact on national affairs. On December 7, 1941, the United States entered World War II on the side of Great Britain and the Soviet Union against Germany, Italy, and Japan. The economic hardships of the Great Depression were left behind as American companies increased their production to support the war effort. Good jobs in defense plants became available to workers. Blacks shared in this prosperity, and Harlem gradually recovered from the nightmare of the 1930s.

Despite the new employment opportunities, discrimination in housing, employment, and education was still highly visible. As councilman, Powell continued to lash out at all racially restricted institutions. He denounced several of the municipal colleges, whose faculty members were all white. He called for the impeachment of Mayor Fiorello La Guardia for sanctioning a segregated housing project. And he pushed for a law forbidding newspapers from identifying the race of suspected criminals. His actions grabbed headlines.

However, Powell did not influence his fellow councilmen; they rejected every measure he proposed. Nevertheless, by disrupting the normal flow of political business, he called attention to injustices, and occasionally a wrong was righted. Within two years of his protest over segregated residential units, the city council outlawed racially restricted public housing. The city's colleges quietly began to integrate their faculties.

The day-to-day work of a city councilman bored Powell. Furthermore, he did not really have time for it. He not only kept a full schedule as the pastor at Abyssinia but helped found a new publication, *The People's Voice*. The newspaper was a daily tabloid replete with photographs and large headlines.

In time, a larger political prize captured Powell's attention. He confided to an associate, "The place to be is not in the city council; they haven't any power to do things for the people of the city." The place to be was Washington, D.C., in Congress. In 1943, the New York state legislature created a congressional district for Harlem, and Powell decided that the position was tailor-made for him. He stepped down from the city council after one term and started his campaign for Congress.

According to Adam Clayton Powell, Sr., the rioting that took place in Harlem on August 1, 1943, was "the hottest hell ever created in Harlem." The rioting left five people dead and hundreds wounded.

As Powell geared up for the race, Harlem suffered through the most violent summer in its history. Early in the evening on Sunday, August 1, 1943, a white policeman shot a black soldier during a dispute at the Hotel Braddock on West 126th Street. As in 1935, ugly rumors spread, and in the sweltering August heat, matters quickly got out of hand. Bands of looters and arsonists roamed the streets, breaking into stores. Thousands of police and soldiers raced to Harlem and attempted to restore order, but peace came only after frightful violence that left 5 dead, 500 injured, 600 arrested, and millions of dollars in property damage.

Powell blamed the violence on blacks' resentment of the mistreatment of black soldiers by the U.S. military and on the high rents charged by white landlords in Harlem. Another factor may well have been

Writer James Baldwin said of the rioting in 1943, "I truly had not realized that Harlem had so many stores until I saw them all smashed open; the first time the word wealth ever entered my mind in relation to Harlem was when I saw it scattered in the streets."

Powell pickets a Harlem store in an effort to win higher wages and shorter working hours for some of his constituents.

the Harlemites' anger about the continued lynching of innocent blacks by white mobs in the South, for the Harlem riot was not an isolated event. During World War II, racial disturbances plagued several other cities. In the aftermath of these riots, Americans came face to face with a sad truth: The United States was fighting oppression in Europe and Asia, but its racial policies at home still condoned much shocking violence.

Early in the war, First Lady Eleanor Roosevelt said, "The nation cannot expect colored people to feel that the United States is worth defending if the Negro continues to be treated as he is now." Most blacks supported the war effort and clamored for a chance to fight for their country. Yet they also called for America to make good on its grand words about freedom and democracy. The front page of Powell's tabloid, *The People's Voice*, was at one time dominated by two giant *V*s. One stood for victory over Germany and its allies; the other *V* stood for victory over segregation.

By 1944, Powell's following in Harlem was so large and strong that the result of the congressional election was a foregone conclusion. No one even seriously opposed him. In the primaries, he won the nomination not only of the Democratic party but of the Republican party and the small, left-wing American Labor party as well. He saw for himself a long and bright future. "The man who gets into Congress from this district," he told a friend, "can stay there for the rest of his life." ◖◗

5

TRIALS OF
A CONGRESSMAN

———— ❦ ————

HARLEM PACKED ITS new congressman off
to Washington, D.C., in December 1944 with a rol-
licking celebration at the Golden Gate ballroom. Amid
the happy throng in the crowded room, Powell glowed.
He was riding the crest of fame and accomplishment,
and he was once more in love. He had fallen for a
strikingly intelligent singer-actress and jazz pianist
named Hazel Scott, who had already appeared in a
half dozen films and was the star attraction at Café
Society, an exclusive Manhattan night spot.

Shortly after Powell's divorce from Isabel became
final in the summer of 1945, he and Hazel were married at a small church in Connecticut, with only a
few friends in attendance.

During the first year of their marriage, Powell and
Hazel Scott lived a storybook life. When not in
Washington, D.C., they divided their time between
Hazel's home in a plush New York suburb and a
summer house on the southern half of Long Island,
at Westhampton, New York. They also kept a spacious apartment in Harlem but seldom saw the grim
streets of the ghetto. More often, they frequented
concerts and Broadway openings or sat at the best
tables in fine restaurants. Powell described his idyllic
existence by saying, "My life with Hazel has been
chock full of the kind of experiences that would excite
the average American husband—warm, golden brown

When the House of Representa-
tives convened in 1945, U.S.
congressmen William Dawson
(left) and Powell were its only
two black members. Although
they possessed different political
styles, both men remained in
Congress for more than 25 years.

Powell's Harlem congregation was used to his bold actions and fast living by the time he remarried in 1945. His first marriage to a nightclub performer had created quite a stir, but his marriage to Hazel Scott (shown here), who was also an entertainer, caused very little concern.

hot cakes on a winter morning; lazy summer afternoons on our Long Island beach; beer and crackers and cheese on our terrace; relaxing evenings at the neighborhood movie house and in the living room before the fire, with Rachmaninoff's Second Piano Concerto coming out of the phonograph."

When Hazel gave birth to a son, Adam Clayton Powell III, in 1946, many people in Harlem celebrated the baby's arrival as if it were a royal birth. They showered presents on the infant and his parents. An admirer sent a gold spoon, saying he always wanted to see a black baby born with one in his mouth. Powell told the press that the child's first words were "Vote for Daddy."

Despite these happy moments, an unhappy incident occurred. The nation's capital had only one large concert auditorium, Constitution Hall, which was owned and controlled by the Daughters of the American Revolution (DAR). When Hazel attempted to book the hall in 1945 for a piano recital, the DAR turned her down because she was black. The organization's racist attitude was well known; in the 1930s, it had denied the hall to Marian Anderson, the black singer. At that time, First Lady Eleanor Roosevelt had castigated the DAR and dropped her membership in the organization. After the incident in which Hazel was turned down by the DAR, President Harry Truman spoke out against the DAR's racism, yet his wife, Bess, went ahead and attended a tea party given by the organization. Hazel's angry husband then said, "From now on there is only one First Lady, Mrs. Roosevelt; Mrs. Truman is the last."

Truman subsequently refused to have any contact with Powell and swore that he would not allow the Harlem congressman to set foot in the White House. For any other freshman Democrat, not being on speaking terms with the president would have been a calamity, but Powell was not just another congressman. He was determined to be the militant, uncom-

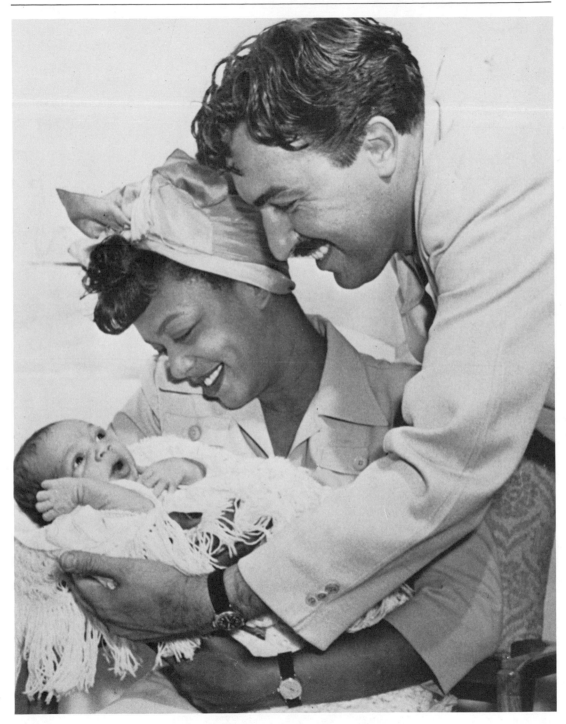

Powell and his second wife, Hazel, with their son, Adam Clayton Powell III.

promising champion of black rights on Capitol Hill. If he offended the Trumans, he thought, too bad. He loved to say, "I'm the first bad nigger in Congress," and he intended to prove it.

Powell spelled out his feelings in a book published in 1945, *Marching Blacks*. The book was part autobiography, part trumpet call for blacks to get "on their feet and marching up Freedom Road." Powell told southern blacks to "pack up and move." Although black life in the North was far from perfect, at least there were no lynchings, and blacks living in a New York or Detroit, Michigan, slum had more opportunities than sharecroppers living in a shack in Mississippi. Come north, he counseled. "It does not

During his tenure in Congress, Powell rarely did things by the book. Noted for his independent ways, he seldom compromised.

matter how you come, brother, but come," he wrote. "Come flying, riding or walking. The great Hegira has begun."

In calling for a *hegira*, or mass exodus, of southern blacks, Powell was stating that blacks would never be given political representation in a section of the country where the majority of them were faced with absurd procedures when it came time to register to vote, were threatened with physical abuse if they did not vote for a certain candidate, were asked to vote only for candidates supported by whites in the primaries, and could not afford to vote because of poll taxes. He put much of the blame for the bitter plight of southern blacks at the feet of the South's white supremacist politicians. He said, "The South will soon learn that some of the men they have sent to the nation's capital have been a disgrace not only to the nation, but to their section as well."

In the halls and on the floor of the House, Powell rubbed shoulders with these very same segregationists. For the most part, they were Democrats, proud members of their party. But Powell did not let party loyalty or the decorum of the House stop him from confronting racism. In particular, he made life miserable for John E. Rankin, a short, white-haired representative from Mississippi. In the opinion of many, Rankin would likely take the prize for the most venomous racist ever to serve in the House. His antipathy to blacks was matched by his extreme hatred of Jews, and his speeches in the House were sprinkled with racial slurs aimed at both groups.

Powell's arrival in Congress had sent Rankin into a fury. William Dawson, a black representative from Chicago, Illinois, had been in Congress since 1942, but he was much less vocal about racism than was Powell. Rankin declared that Powell's presence in the House was a "disgrace," and said he would not "let Adam C. Powell sit by me." Powell responded in kind: "I'm happy that Rankin won't sit by me because that makes it mutual." He stated that the only people who deserved to sit next to the Mississippi congressman were Adolf Hitler and Benito Mussolini.

Powell could not resist the temptation to make his presence even more annoying to Rankin. "Whenever Rankin entered the chamber," he recounted, "I followed after him, sitting next to him or as close as I could. One day the press reported that he moved five times."

If Powell enraged Rankin, he also irritated his natural allies, the liberal Democrats in Congress. For one thing, Powell had a very poor congressional attendance record. Rather than attend tedious discussions in the House, he frequently took trips away from the capital with little explanation of what he was doing. But the liberal congressmen were especially displeased by his constant use of a legislative device that served to keep the issue of racial discrimination in the public eye. It became known as the Powell amendment.

Powell first used the device on June 4, 1946, when he proposed an amendment to a bill providing federal funds for free lunches for schoolchildren. His amendment barred states from excluding black children from the program. At the time, no state legislature had any intention of limiting the food fund assistance to white children, and the bill with its attached amendment passed. With this victory under his belt, Powell realized he had hit on a weapon against segregation. He wondered what would happen if he offered a similar amendment to other measures. Powell was a member of the House Committee on Education and Labor, which concerned itself with funding for schools and employment programs, and he decided to attach an amendment to education bills that would prevent federal funds from being spent in any state that practiced segregation.

What happened was havoc. In the 1950s, Powell introduced his amendment to nearly every bill providing federal aid for education. To be sure, denying funds to states having segregated schools was both right and just. The legality of segregated schools had long been questioned, and in the monumental *Brown v. Board of Education* decision of 1954, the Supreme Court declared them unconstitutional. President Dwight D. Eisenhower, who led the Republican party to victory in the 1952 elections, privately admitted "that in view of the Supreme Court decision, a vote against Powell would seem to be a vote against the Constitution." However, until well into the 1960s, the South resisted every attempt to integrate its schools, and southern congressmen refused to support any bill that included the Powell amendment. Without southern votes in Congress, federal aid to education was doomed.

Liberal congressmen were in a difficult position. If they supported Powell, federal funding for schools would be lost. On the other hand, if they helped to push through bills without the Powell amendment, they would be abandoning their commitment to civil rights. Adlai Stevenson, the Democratic presidential candidate in 1952 and 1956, did not back the Powell amendment. "The objective of such an amendment," he said, "seems entirely plausible and proper but we musn't hazard the loss of the whole program to serve an objective such as that. The important thing is education."

Powell was immune to such logic. He attached his amendment to bill after bill and watched federal support for education suffer. "I am an irritant," he explained. "I rub until something gives. All my strength, all my money, comes from Negroes, and therefore I cannot be controlled by whites."

Once, during a session of the House Education and Labor Committee, Powell rubbed a colleague

A man of many worlds, Powell was as at home attending a formal affair in a black tie and tuxedo as he was in the pulpit at Abyssinia.

A black worker in Jackson, Mississippi, paints segregation signs under the watchful eyes of a city employee. As a member of Congress, Powell was a leader in the fight against segregation.

beyond endurance. When he introduced his amendment to a $1.6 billion school construction bill, Representative Cleveland Bailey of West Virginia could stand it no longer. Powell was insincere, Bailey screamed, and he was trying to wreck the whole public school system. "You're a liar," retorted Powell. With that, the 69-year-old Bailey rushed the tall New Yorker and uncorked a punch that caught Powell on the jaw, sending him sprawling. "Restrain your passions, gentlemen," shouted the committee chairman, and Powell did not retaliate. Later, he and Bailey patched up their differences. "Cleve Bailey and I smoked cigars together and are old friends," he told reporters.

These squabbles on Capitol Hill only added to his popularity in Harlem. His defiance of rich, powerful congressmen struck a responsive chord in a community of poor, powerless blacks. In his first reelection campaign in 1946, he bragged that he had called a southern senator a "rat." Before cheering Harlem crowds, he launched a blistering attack on his black Republican opponent, calling him a servile "Uncle Tom" and "the darling of the big Negroes who hate the little Negroes." He did not try to hide his poor attendance record in the House. After all, he asked, who among his constituents would deny him and Hazel Scott their honeymoon after the 1945 wedding? He coasted to an easy victory. It would be followed by many more triumphant elections. By the 1960s, he would be boasting that he could win with "Mickey Mouse as my campaign manager."

Yet Powell ran into some difficulties as well. Some officials in the U.S. Department of Justice, the branch of the federal government that investigates criminal misconduct, wondered whether Powell was cheating on his taxes in order to live so well. In 1952, they charged that he had underestimated his income for 1945 by several thousand dollars. After some arguing,

Powell wrote the government a check for $1,193 to cover his back taxes.

That was just the beginning of Powell's troubles. Throughout the 1950s, the Internal Revenue Service and the Justice Department steadily built a case against him. They started by digging into the affairs of his aides. In 1954, the government brought suit against Hattie Freeman Dodson, one of Powell's secretaries. After Dodson confessed that she could not account for large parts of her salary, she was convicted of tax evasion and sentenced to seven months in prison. During the trial, a witness testified that much of Dodson's salary had been returned under the table to Powell. The congressman vehemently denied receiving these kickbacks, and a grand jury found insufficient evidence to indict him.

Rosa Parks is fingerprinted by the police in Montgomery, Alabama, after being arrested for refusing to give up her seat to a white rider on a public bus. Her actions helped awaken the nation to the injustice of segregation.

During this period, Powell began to drift apart from Hazel Scott, who disliked Washington, D.C., and the decorous ways that were expected of a congressional wife. Although she stood up for her husband when reporters asked her about his romantic affairs, by the mid-1950s she and Powell were living apart. He resided in New York and Washington, D.C., while she lived in Paris pursuing her career as an entertainer. Their son spent time with both parents.

Powell did not spend all of his time bickering with politicians, fighting off the Internal Revenue Service, or dealing with family problems. In April 1955, the representatives of 29 newly independent nations met in Bandung, Indonesia. These nations, principally from Asia and Africa, accounted for half the world's population, and at Bandung they met to form the Third World movement, proclaiming their support for racial equality and committing themselves to helping colonial states achieve independence. They also backed a policy of nonalignment in the global

In 1955, delegates from Third World nations met in Bandung, Indonesia. Although the United States did not send any official observers to the meeting, Powell attended the proceedings.

struggle between the Soviet Union and the United States, preferring to remain outside the camps of either superpower.

The U.S. government, on the other hand, wanted the Third World nations to take a strong anticommunist stance. When it became clear prior to the meeting that the delegates at Bandung would not support the U.S. position, the Eisenhower administration decided not to send any official observers there.

Powell thought that this decision was a terrible mistake. He urged the administration to send a delegation to observe the conference. When the State Department again said no, he decided to go himself. He described it as a religious imperative, feeling that the conference would be of supreme worldwide significance. "Bandung was a pilgrimage to a new Mecca," he said. "I was one of the pilgrims and I went because I had to. Divine compulsion had been laid upon me."

When Powell arrived in Indonesia, he was snubbed by the American ambassador and his embassy. He shrugged off this discourtesy and proceeded to engage in some remarkably effective diplomacy. Working at the periphery of the conference, he listened sympathetically to the Asian and African delegates, and he stood up for the United States against the concerted attacks of the representatives of the Communist powers.

The delegates from China and the journalists from other Communist countries were determined to spread anti-American feeling in Bandung. They hoped that the conference would endorse a resolution condemning the United States for its racial policies. Powell, the unyielding foe of segregation, took the offensive. At a press conference, he acknowledged that racism was still strong in America, but he insisted that great progress was being made. A journalist from Poland inquired about the mistreatment of blacks in South Carolina. "Let's not judge the United States by what is happening in its worst states," Powell replied, "but let's judge it by what is happening in most of its states and use this as a goal to clean up the rest of the country." Hearing this from America's most outspoken black politician, the New York *Herald-Tribune* reported, "the communist correspondents put away their notebooks in sneering disgust."

Thanks in part to Powell's work at Bandung, the delegates from the Communist nations failed to gather much support for their anti-American campaign. When Powell returned to Washington, D.C., a few of his colleagues in Congress applauded his statesmanship, and President Eisenhower later thanked him privately.

Following Powell's triumphant debut in international diplomacy, new inquiries into his financial affairs began. In 1956, another of his aides, Acy Lennon, was charged with tax evasion. The trial revolved around some shady transactions in Harlem real estate in which Powell had an interest. The prosecution demanded to see records about the deal that were supposedly in Powell's possession, but he claimed that the records no longer existed. He explained that some had been carried off by playful children, some destroyed by fire, and others stolen. Again, Powell escaped being indicted, but Lennon was convicted, fined, and sent to jail for a year and a day. Powell called the judgment "the rawest deal a man ever got." Obviously, federal officials were intent on examining Powell's affairs, but he was an elusive target.

Just after Lennon's conviction in the fall of 1956, Powell exploded a political bombshell. On October 12, he spent a half hour at the White House with President Eisenhower. They evidently had a pleasant meeting because Powell announced to reporters as he stepped from the Oval Office that as a Democrat with 12 years of service in the House, he was endorsing Eisenhower, the Republican candidate, for president in the upcoming elections.

The Democrats feared that Powell might persuade millions of blacks to abandon their allegiance to the party of Franklin Roosevelt and the New Deal. Powell offered several reasons for refusing to support the Democratic party's candidate. He said that Adlai Stevenson, the Democratic nominee, was weak on civil rights and opposed the use of the Powell amendment. Powell was right: Stevenson had tried to keep the northern and southern wings of the party together by equivocating on civil rights. But what did Powell expect to gain from Eisenhower? By and large, the president was even less sympathetic to blacks than Stevenson.

The Democrats immediately assumed Powell had cut a deal. They suspected that he had agreed to endorse the president's reelection if the Justice Department would drop its investigation into whether or not he had evaded paying enough income tax. Eleanor Roosevelt, while campaigning for Stevenson,

Adlai Stevenson, the Democratic candidate for president in 1952 and 1956, refused to support Powell's attempts to ban segregation from all pieces of legislation. Stevenson's refusal prompted Powell—and many black voters— to support Dwight Eisenhower, a Republican candidate, for the presidential bid in the mid-1950s.

In a magazine article entitled "Death of an Investigation: The Wheels of Justice Stop for Adam Clayton Powell, Jr.," National Review editor William F. Buckley, Jr., insisted that the Eisenhower administration had, as a political favor, called off a federal investigation of Powell.

accused Powell of "accepting promises of some kind, of benefit to him, but not his people."

Although at the time of the election no evidence was presented against Powell or Eisenhower, many people continued to ask whether or not the two had struck a deal. In the months following Eisenhower's victory, it certainly appeared that a deal had been made. The Justice Department shut down the Powell investigation, dismissed a grand jury that was reviewing evidence against him, and transferred the chief prosecutor, Thomas A. Bolan, to other business. Embittered, Bolan resigned from the department. But he did not keep quiet. He told his side of the story to William F. Buckley, Jr., the editor of a new conservative magazine, *National Review*. In December 1957, Buckley published an article entitled "Death of an Investigation: The Wheels of Justice Stop for Adam Clayton Powell, Jr." The piece claimed that Bolan had uncovered enough evidence to indict Powell for tax evasion but his superiors had told the prosecutor that the case was "too hot to handle."

The *National Review* article rekindled interest in Powell's finances, and the Justice Department reassembled its case. A new prosecutor presented the evidence to the grand jury, and on May 8, 1958, Powell was indicted for tax evasion. Wisely, he retained for his defense one of the best lawyers in the business, Edward Bennett Williams.

The trial finally convened on March 18, 1960, in the federal courthouse in New York. Some matters that were embarrassing to Powell were brought to light at the trial. He had overstepped the line of the law by taking tax deductions for his liquor bills, tele-

When Powell was indicted for tax evasion in May 1958, he was represented by Edward Bennett Williams (right), one of the nation's most respected attorneys.

Jurists hearing the Justice Department's case of income tax evasion against Powell leave the New York federal courthouse in 1960. The lively trial, which ran for six weeks, ended with Powell's acquittal.

vision sets, and repair work done on his boats. But as the trial progressed, it became obvious that no political deal had been struck four years before. Rather, the Justice Department probably had dropped the case simply because it was full of holes.

For six weeks, the trial was one of the best shows in town. Powell's quick wit and Williams's courtroom theatrics made a shambles of the prosecution. While testifying on his own behalf, Powell was asked if he had deducted the cost of his son's private school tuition. "Sure," he said, "everybody knows that Adam Clayton Powell is for federal aid to education." Even the judge laughed at the remark. What Powell could not handle with humor, Williams took care of with figures. At one point, the lawyer got a government accountant to admit that perhaps Powell had *overestimated* his income and paid too much in taxes.

Williams pulled out all the stops in his appeal to the jury. Powell was not on trial for his tax returns, Williams said, but for his political beliefs. The high and the mighty were out to get him. He begged the jury to render a verdict that would "give thundering notice that there is no room for political trials in this land."

The jury deliberated and quarreled for 26 hours. One juror had a gall bladder attack; another became hysterical. Exhausted, they filed back before the judge and admitted that they were hopelessly divided. The vote stood at 10 to 2, in favor of Powell's acquittal. The case was dismissed.

Powell and his supporters were jubilant. In Harlem, a prayer meeting of thanksgiving was held at Abyssinia. A while later, Powell gave Williams a large gold trophy. To the crowd gathered on the steps of the Hotel Theresa in Harlem he said, "I give you a man who is greater than Abraham Lincoln. Abraham Lincoln freed the slaves, but Edward Bennett Williams freed Adam Clayton Powell." ❧

6

MR. CHAIRMAN

❧

O N A STEAMING August evening in 1958, the Carver Ballroom was swarming with Harlemites. The center of attention was their handsome, 6-foot 3-inch, 190-pound congressman. Powell stood near a wall, sipping a Scotch, smiling and laughing as well-wishers pressed in, anxious to shake his hand, to slap his back, to offer congratulations. He had just scored the biggest political triumph of his career. He had beaten Tammany Hall.

Tammany was New York's Democratic organization, its political machine. Since the early 1800s, Tammany's leaders had controlled city hall and won an unsavory reputation for graft and corruption. But years of scandals had exacted a toll, and by the 1950s Tammany was a shadow of its former self. Nevertheless, its leader, Carmine DeSapio, still had muscles to flex. In 1958, he decided to teach Congressman Powell a lesson.

The party leaders at Tammany had a long string of scores to settle with Powell, going back to his days on the city council. They detested his independence and his unwillingness to cooperate with the Democratic organization in New York and Washington, D.C. Like the party's leaders in Congress, they re-

Powell and some of his supporters at the Abyssinian Baptist Church celebrate his reelection to Congress in 1958.

73

sented the Powell amendment and the threat it posed to federal aid to schools. Federal education assistance was an important issue to New York voters. But Powell's endorsement of Eisenhower for reelection in 1956 had been the last straw. Not only did he back the president, he campaigned for some Republican candidates for Congress. Partly as a result, the Republicans had sliced into Harlem's usually enormous Democratic vote margins.

Yet DeSapio believed that Powell was losing his hold on Harlem. Surely, he reasoned, Powell's flamboyance, his taste for the high life, his poor attendance in the House, his tax troubles—all had made him an embarrassment to his district. DeSapio concluded that he would purge Powell from the party in the 1958 elections. His strategy was simple: He would support another candidate in the Democratic primary, throw all of Tammany's organization behind the candidate, and send the troublemaking Powell crashing to defeat.

Tammany's choice of a candidate to run against Powell was Earl Brown, an impressive, Harvard-educated man who was an editor for *Life* magazine. For years, he had worked quietly for civil rights as Harlem's representative on the city council, but when DeSapio told him he was Tammany's choice to oppose Powell, Brown was startled. "Why me?" he asked.

It was a question he must have muttered again and again as the campaign unfolded. Opposing Powell in Harlem was a fool's errand. DeSapio had totally misread public opinion; above 110th Street, where the district of Harlem began, Powell had never been more popular. Tammany's attempted purge only added to Powell's appeal because Harlem instinctively distrusted the city's "downtown bosses." The widespread support for Powell was reflected by one Harlemite who said, "I never voted for him before, but I'm going to this time."

Determined to defeat the organization, Powell waged his most active campaign in years, charging about his district, swinging his deadliest punches. "I am being purged by Carmine DeSapio because I am a Negro, and a Negro should stay on the plantation," he boomed. While riding through the streets of Harlem in his campaign sound truck, he ridiculed his opponent, "Lookdown Brown," as an "Uncle Tom," the slave of "Massa DeSapio."

On the Saturday before the balloting, Powell brought the campaign to a climax before thousands of supporters in front of the Hotel Theresa in Harlem. The popular bandleader Dizzy Gillespie and his musicians warmed up the rally with throbbing jazz choruses. When Powell took the microphone, he was at his rabble-rousing best. With his silk shirt half un-

Carmine DeSapio, the head of the Democratic party in New York, sought to punish Powell for his political independence by promoting another Democrat, Earl Brown, for Congress in the 1958 elections.

buttoned, his chest gleaming with sweat, he held the crowd spellbound for a half hour, his voice falling to a velvet whisper or rising to an impassioned shout. At last, he cried out, "I appeal to your manhood! Harlem is on the march!" He smiled, waved, and departed, leaving tumult and cheers behind.

Three days later, Harlem showed that its heart still belonged to Powell. The results in the Democratic primary were 14,935 votes for Powell and 4,959 votes for Brown. "We will drive the Uncle Toms from Harlem," Powell promised. "Carmine will have to pay the price," he said, threatening Tammany with further attacks. He took a quick tour of the district in his sound truck, thanked the voters, and then departed for a holiday in the Caribbean.

Powell looks over a list he had made public that names people and places in New York City allegedly involved in illegal gambling operations. In 1960, he also publicly accused a Harlem woman of paying off the local police—an accusation that he would later regret.

Powell's difficulties with the Democratic party were not limited to the North. The southern Democrats held an extremely strong position in Congress in the 1950s, and their voters back home hated Powell with a passion. For a southern congressman, any association with Powell was poison. In the deep recesses of the Capitol, Powell and his southern colleagues laughed and drank together, but they were never seen together in public.

None of the congressmen could forget what had happened to Jim Folsom, the hospitable governor of Alabama. In 1955, Folsom invited Powell to the governor's mansion in Montgomery for a drink. When Alabama's white population heard about the meeting, they erupted. As late as 1958, a southern journalist wrote: "Folsom has gotten away with a lot of things in and out of public office, but having a drink with Powell is as fresh on the minds of the people now as it was two and one-half years ago. For this he may never be pardoned."

Representative Graham Barden of North Carolina, the chairman of the House Committee on Education and Labor, was not about to make the same mistake. Powell had served on the committee since coming to Congress, but Barden exerted absolute power on the panel. He sometimes announced decisions about education matters without calling a meeting among committee members to discuss the issue. Yet he was a friendly, affable man, and his endless supply of folksy stories placated most members. He was genial to everybody but Powell. He hated the congressman from Harlem with unbridled rage. Powell once told a reporter:

> For six years Barden was intentionally rude to me in public. The chairman presides over committee meetings flanked by ranking Democrats and ranking Republicans. When the chairman finishes, he yields to the next ranking Democrat so on down the line. I was

the next ranking Democrat, but Barden used to look right through me and ask the third ranking Democrat, "Got anything to say, Mr. Bailey?" Then after every one of the thirty members, Democrats and Republicans, had spoken, I would say, "Can I say something, Mr. Barden?" and he would say, "Yes, briefly."

Much of Congress's preparatory work is done in the committees, and all congressmen are members of at least one committee. However, Barden gave Powell virtually nothing to do. The chairman refused to make Powell the head of any subcommittees, which give special attention to one of the committee's areas of investigation. Usually tightfisted in authorizing funds for travels by committee members, he made an exception for Powell. "He let Powell go anywhere," another committee member recalled. "The more Powell was out of town, the better Barden liked it."

The one thing Barden could not control was the system of congressional seniority. The chairmanship of a House or Senate committee goes to the senior committee member of the party in power in Congress, which except between 1953 and 1955 was the Democrats. Year after year, Powell won reelection, and he maintained his rather loose affiliation with the Democratic party. At the committee's table, where seats are assigned by seniority, Powell's place moved closer and closer to the chairman's. Finally, Barden and Powell sat side by side. Several times, Barden postponed retirement so that Powell would not inherit the chairmanship, but in 1960 an old and tired Barden gave up and went back to North Carolina. When the new Congress convened in January 1961, Powell was chairman of the Committee on Education and Labor, a powerful position.

In the meantime, a small cloud had appeared on Powell's horizon. It quickly grew into a terrible, destructive storm. In March 1960, Senator Hubert Humphrey was unable to travel to New York for his scheduled appearance on "Between the Lines," a television interview program. Powell graciously filled in, and the show went well. He was talkative and informative as usual, and he repeated a charge he had made the month before in a House speech: The New York Police Department was riddled with corruption. When asked by the interviewer to be more specific, Powell obliged by citing a Harlem woman, 70-year-old Esther James, as a "bag woman for the Police Department." In other words, he was saying that James passed bribes and graft from local criminals to police officers.

James said that she was innocent of such a charge and demanded an apology. Powell ignored her, so she engaged an attorney, filed a defamation of character suit against the congressman, and asked for $1 million in damages. When given a chance to settle out of court, Powell continued to ignore James and her attorney. He was confident that this small cloud would blow over and that the case would disappear.

In December 1960, a month after Powell's divorce from Hazel was final, he married Yvette Marjorie Flores Diago in Puerto Rico. They had met in Puerto Rico several years earlier on a blind date. Yvette subsequently came to Washington, D.C., and joined Powell's staff as a secretary. When the newlyweds returned from their honeymoon, they settled into a comfortable white stucco townhouse in Washington, D.C. However, Yvette was not in the capital much and visited the Abyssinian Baptist Church in Harlem only once.

Yvette preferred to live in Puerto Rico, where Powell built a lavish 6-room beach house, Villa Reposo, 20 miles outside San Juan. His wife remained on the congressional payroll and was even given a raise. She translated letters from Powell's Spanish-speaking constituents, the congressman explained, sometimes as many as 20 or 25 a day. On most weekends, he flew to his wife on the island for a few days of sun on the beach.

Esther James leaves a New York courthouse in 1963 in the midst of her eight-year-long legal battle with Powell. Her suit originated when Powell called her a collector of graft and bribes for police in Harlem.

Perhaps as a result of these trends in Powell's life, few were happy with his rise to the chairmanship of the committee on Education and Labor. George Meany, an important labor union official, expressed a typical view: "Terrible." The *New York Times*, then as now the editorial voice of mainstream liberalism, shuddered at the prospect of Powell wielding a chairman's gavel: "The racist attitudes of Adam Clayton Powell, his miserable record as a legislator, and his extreme absenteeism all tend to disqualify him as a responsible and effective chairman."

Within a short while, Powell made his critics eat their words. Eleanor Roosevelt, who in the past had spoken out against Powell, wrote to a friend, "I have to own that Mr. Powell is proving a good chairman of his committee." For the first year of his tenure, he was that and more. He assembled a large, professional staff, fairly distributed committee business to the other members, and conducted crisp, regular meetings. He did what many had thought impossible: He decided to become a team player. To help push federal aid to education bills through the House, he dropped his use of the Powell amendment. Even the Republicans were impressed. "What more can you ask of a chairman," said one congressman.

For a change, Powell had a friend in the White House. On January 20, 1961, John F. Kennedy became president and brought with him an agenda of liberal reform, the New Frontier. Kennedy had served in the House with Powell and genuinely liked him. He also had important business to do with Powell and needed to be on the best of terms with the chairman of the House Committee on Education and Labor.

The president carefully stroked and flattered Powell. Discussing his close association with Kennedy, Powell once said, "He would never have his secretary call me but would always telephone directly." Powell was a frequent guest at Kennedy's glittering White House entertainments. As usual, he was irrepressible.

He loyally shepherded New Frontier legislation through his committee and onto the House floor for voting. Laws were passed to increase the minimum wage, establish programs for vocational training, and provide education benefits for handicapped citizens.

Still, storm clouds continued to build. In July 1962, Yvette gave birth to a son, Adam Clayton Powell-Diago, who was called Adamcito by his parents. Powell's weekends in Puerto Rico frequently stretched into the greater part of a week. He had never been a stickler for answering roll calls in the House, and now that he was a committee chairman, his attendance record stayed poor. "You don't have to be there if you know which calls to make, which buttons to push, which favors to call in," he said. He also took advantage of the tempting opportunities

Powell proved to be an influential supporter of Democratic candidate John F. Kennedy during his successful bid for the presidency in 1960. Another influential Democrat, former first lady Eleanor Roosevelt, is shown at right.

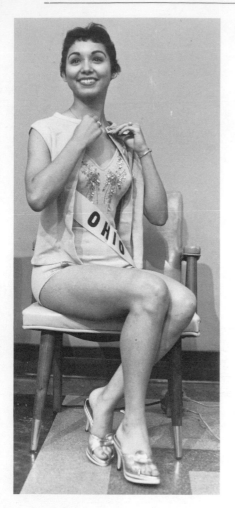

Corinne Huff, the first black to win the title of Miss Ohio, accompanied Powell to Europe in 1962 when he went to investigate job opportunities for women. By the mid-1960s, she had become a steady companion.

that congressmen had to travel at the taxpayer's expense. Every summer for two decades, he toured Europe, supposedly to investigate some aspect of continental life or American foreign relations. More to the point, these trips allowed him to be a regular at social events such as the Salzburg Music Festival in Austria and at ringside tables in Paris nightclubs.

At one point during the summer of 1962, it appeared that he would have to miss his European excursion. At an August press conference in New York, he talked about the amount of business he had to take care of back in Washington, D.C. Not only was his committee about to examine the affairs of a labor union, he said, but the House would be considering legislation for a constitutional amendment to outlaw the poll tax, a device that some southern states used to deny the ballot to impoverished blacks who could not pay voting registration fees.

The cruise liner *Queen Mary* was sailing that afternoon for Europe, and a reporter asked Powell if he was going to be a passenger on the ship. The congressman said no. He had made a reservation on the ship, but Congress was so busy, he had canceled it.

A little more than an hour later, Powell marched up the ship's gangplank and began a month's tour of Europe. He was going to investigate employment opportunities for women in Common Market countries. Two members of his staff sailed with him: Corrine Huff, his receptionist, a stunning woman who in 1960 had been the first black Miss Ohio, and Tamara J. Wall, a divorcée on the Education and Labor committee's staff.

The result of the European research was never unveiled. However, Powell amply demonstrated his taste for grand hotels, three-star restaurants, and exotic nightclubs. In Washington, D.C., congressmen waging the difficult battle against the poll tax seethed at Powell's desertion. The *New York Times* thundered against the "frivolous junket," writing that "the reck-

less, irresponsible conduct of Mr. Powell is a disgrace." In Puerto Rico, his wife, purportedly still answering mail, shot off an angry cable to Europe, which stated that he should return home.

Powell left his staff in Madrid, Spain, and hurried to Puerto Rico. At the airport in San Juan, he kissed and embraced both Yvette and Adamcito as photographer and reporters caught the scene. Powell obviously had some explaining to do, but he was good at that. Months later, Yvette said: "Adam Clayton Powell is surely one of the most persuasive men on earth. To this day, despite all our troubles, I believe

Powell greets his third wife, Yvette, in Puerto Rico after returning from Europe with two female members of his staff. He received a great deal of criticism for going on a junket while Congress was considering important legislation.

that if I were looking at a white wall and he assured me it was red, I would look again and be half convinced it was indeed red."

Powell's colleagues were not so forgiving. Senator John Williams of Delaware abandoned congressional courtesy and attacked Powell by name on the Senate floor. In the House, there was talk of dividing Education and Labor into two committees. "They're trying to split the Adam," Powell joked. Worst of all, when he at last returned to the House chamber some of his colleagues laughed and snickered at him for the very first time. Powell called in the press and testily pointed out that his fellow congressmen were just as adept in dubious trips as he was. "I'm not going to enjoy any more privileges than by the Grace of God any other congressman," he said, "but I'm not going to take any less either."

President Lyndon Johnson signs a landmark piece of legislation—the Civil Rights Act of 1964. The bill was designed to eliminate segregation in public places and offer equal employment opportunities to all Americans.

In the spring of 1963, Esther James's case against Powell finally came to trial. However, he refused to appear in court, and his lawyers were left with a lame defense. The jury deliberated for four hours, found for James, and awarded her $211,000. She was beside herself with joy, saying, "The king is dead! Adam Clayton Powell is dead! And the respectable people will be able to walk in the streets again!" However, she still had to collect her money.

The affair degenerated into a incredible tug-of-war between a determined, elderly Harlem woman and a headstrong congressman. As James continued to file suits, the case passed through 10 separate courts for appeals and came before 80 different judges. But the basic judgment never changed. The appellate courts upheld the original jury's decision, though they reduced what Powell owed to James.

While all of this was happening in Powell's private life, a coalition of Republicans and conservative Democrats was blocking Kennedy's most ambitious aims. Ironically, the assassination of the president on November 22, 1963, helped break the congressional logjam. Lyndon B. Johnson, a master of legislative give-and-take, succeeded to the presidency and swiftly took advantage of the popular support for the social reform program that grew in the aftermath of the Kennedy assassination.

Powell did not socialize with the Johnsons as he had with the Kennedys, but he got on well with Johnson, whose unsuccessful bid for the Democratic presidential nomination in 1960 had been supported by Powell. A lobbyist recalled stopping by Powell's office late one afternoon for a drink. As they were discussing legislation, the phone rang. It was President Johnson. Powell smiled, reclined in his leather chair, and propped his feet on the desk; holding his drink in one hand and cradling the telephone in the other, he spoke as though he were speaking to one of his female admirers: "Hello, baby!" The lobbyist

Powell addresses a crowd in Harlem during a rally for equal rights. He told his constituents that blacks "should all work together and fight together and boycott together."

heard the burst of presidential laughter at the other end of the line.

Johnson took Kennedy's New Frontier and, with his Texan flair, turned it into a social program that he called the "Great Society." Between 1963 and 1968, he scored the most important series of victories for social welfare legislation since the New Deal of Franklin Roosevelt. In June 1964, the president signed a civil rights bill that prohibited racially discriminatory employment practices and the segregation of public places such as restaurants and train stations. In August 1965, a voting rights bill was enacted that barred racially biased voting registration practices. Other legislation provided federally funded Medicare assistance to the elderly, increased aid for education, established government programs to help relieve poverty, and supported housing and urban development programs.

Meanwhile, James's legal battle against Powell continued to rage on. To avoid having the courts seize his assets, he transferred them out of New York, then hid them in dummy corporations. When he refused to be questioned about these transactions, the courts issued contempt citations against him, first civil, then criminal. The criminal citations meant that he could be arrested in New York, and he therefore stopped coming to the city.

Matters remained that way in November 1966, when Powell was reelected to Congress by his usual smashing margin. However, if he tried to come to New York to thank the voters, he would very likely be arrested. He had chosen to flaunt the law and was, in a sense, a fugitive from justice.

In Washington, D.C., however, Powell continued to be a vital cog in the congressional machine that manufactured the Great Society. Johnson praised the chairman for his "brilliant record of accomplishment" and pointed to 49 pieces of important legislation that Powell had guided through Education and Labor. "And the passage of every one of these bills attests to your ability to get things done," said the president of the United States.

Despite some personal turmoil, the early 1960s was Powell's political heyday. ❧

7

A DEFIANT
FUGITIVE

— ❦ —

THE AIR IN Washington, D.C., on August 28, 1963, was filled with hope and dignity. A quarter million blacks and whites paraded from the Washington Monument to the Lincoln Memorial during the Great March on Washington for Jobs and Freedom. Baptists and Jews, Catholics and Methodists, autoworkers and farmers proceeded down Constitution and Independence avenues carrying placards calling for an end to racial discrimination. It was a joyous day. The civil rights movement—the crusade of blacks and whites working together for equality— was at full tide. Even as the marchers carried their message to Washington, D.C., Congress was considering a sweeping new civil rights law.

At the Lincoln Memorial, speaker after speaker addressed the crowds that spread as far as the eye could see. Finally, the movement's most prominent leader rose and spoke. "I have a dream," said Martin Luther King, Jr. "Dream some more," the crowd responded. "Free at last! Free at last!" he cried. "Thank God Almighty, we are free at last!"

Now and then during the long afternoon of speechmaking, a voice in the crowd would shout, "Let Powell speak!" or "Where's Adam?" Powell was there, nearly out of sight, sitting on an uncomfortable folding chair, puffing his pipe. Occasionally, he applauded, but he did not speak. The organizers of the

On August 28, 1963, more than 250,000 people from all over America marched in the nation's capital, from the Washington Monument to the Lincoln Memorial, in a demonstration for the advancement of civil rights.

March on Washington, the leaders of the civil rights movement, wanted nothing to do with him. Recent statements by the congressman about racial politics had completely alienated the more moderate civil rights leaders.

Also in town that day watching the march was Malcolm X, a dynamic, charismatic leader of the militant Black Muslim movement. He derided the parade as the "Farce on Washington," something "weakening, lulling, deluding" black Americans. If Martin Luther King, Jr., spoke of a dream, Malcolm X dealt in nightmares. The gruesome plight of blacks in America, he said, could not be remedied by integration; whites were still slave masters, could never be trusted, and must be shunned. King preached non-violence and sought to ally the different races in a movement of social and political reform. Malcolm X called for revolutionary black separatism. He was contemptuous of the blacks and whites who marched together in the nation's capital.

In the early 1960s, Powell embraced the black separatist views of militant leader Malcolm X (right). This was a departure for Powell, who had called for blacks and whites to work together for civil rights when he first entered politics.

Between Martin Luther King, Jr., and Malcolm X, there was the clearest of choices: integration or black nationalism. Astonishingly, Powell had turned his back on King and had befriended Malcolm X and the Black Muslims. On a chilly spring day in March 1963, at Seventh Avenue and 125th Street in Harlem, he had shared a platform with Malcolm X. More than 3,000 people had heard their congressman say:

> We Negroes are not going to get anything more in this life except that which we fight for and fight for with all our power. . . . This may sound like black nationalism. If it is, then what is wrong with it? Why is it that racism and nationalism are only dirty words when applied to Negro people? What the white man fears is the coming together of Negroes.

His voice strained with anger, Powell had condemned white involvement in the civil rights movement: "Unless we can seize completely the administration and policy making of our national Negro organizations, then we must say there is no hope for us." Black rights, he had said, would only be won by groups "totally owned, controlled and maintained by Negro people."

Powell's speech provoked a storm of criticism. Nearly every civil rights leader spoke out against him. Whitney Young, head of the National Urban League, complained that "when the whole world is crying for and working toward unity, it comes as a terrible shock to hear the voice of the person of Congressman Powell's stature sowing the seeds of racial discord."

During his first terms in Congress years before, Powell had sung a different tune. At that time, he had attacked a civil rights organization for excluding whites. For civil rights to be won, he had said, white support was vital.

So how did he come to stand arm in arm with Malcolm X? Some of his critics in the civil rights movement suspected that he acted out of personal pique. For years he had shown little interest in their

Civil rights leader Martin Luther King, Jr., was the last speaker at the March on Washington in 1963. He told the crowd, "I have a dream that my four little children will one day live in a nation where they will not be judged by the color of their skin, but by the content of their character."

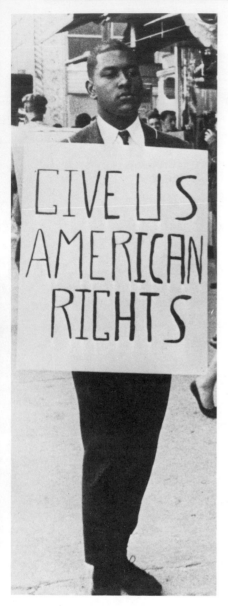

A black student picketing for desegregation and racial equality is shadowed by an unwelcoming white youth (on opposite page) in Greensboro, North Carolina.

organizations, and they, in turn, had excluded him from their deliberations. True, Powell had never been one to follow the lead of others; in fact, it had been said that Powell thought NAACP stood for National Association for Adam Clayton Powell. But by the early 1960s, these organizations—and Martin Luther King, Jr., in particular—had assumed a powerful presence in American life. Ironically, the congressman from Harlem was now a small player in a large drama, just at the time when his influence in the House of Representatives was at its greatest. Bitterly, he called the man whose nonviolent protest had awakened the nation's conscience "Martin Loser King." The only way Powell could salve his ego and recapture the spotlight was by doing something startling, and in 1963 there were few things more audacious than endorsing Malcolm X.

Perhaps the whole affair was an ego trip, a product of Powell's insatiable desire for center stage. But in his own way, he was prophetic. In the half dozen years following the March on Washington, the civil rights movement succeeded. Congress approved landmark legislation, southern blacks won full citizenship rights, and police dogs and fire hoses were no longer turned on black demonstrators. Still, the lives of many blacks did not improve. The long, hot summers of the 1960s saw the ghettos of northern cities—all of them plagued by poverty, joblessness, and crime—erupt into frightful riots. Picking up the pieces, blacks discovered that their erstwhile liberal white allies were nowhere to be found. Their search for economic equality and for better jobs, housing, and schools unfortunately pitted them against some of the very whites who had marched with King.

Whatever Powell's motives, whatever his vision, the endorsements of Malcolm X did him no good. From then on, the organized civil rights movement gave him a cold shoulder. In their view, and in the view of liberal whites, Powell had stamped himself a black racist, dangerous and untrustworthy.

If the rebuff from the black leadership wounded him, he did not let it show. He continued life with the gusto and cheer that once caused a fellow in Harlem, seeing him race by in his Jaguar, to say, "Man, that cat is living."

However, by the end of 1966, things had been sliding downhill in Powell's life for some time. His defiance of the courts in New York tore the last shreds of tolerance in Washington, D.C. He had never been well liked or trusted in the House, but for years his colleagues had let him go his own way. However, his flaunting of the law in the Esther James case and his evasion of a criminal contempt charge was too much for most congressmen to stomach.

A House committee headed by Congressman Wayne Hays of Ohio began to probe a most vulnerable subject, Powell's office payroll. To no one's great surprise, the committee members discovered that quite a lot of money was being paid to people who did very little work. Yvette Powell was drawing an annual salary of more than $20,000 for staying in Puerto Rico. Corrine Huff, his European companion of 1962, was being paid $19,300 a year and yet was almost never in the office. Actually, this was old news to many of Powell's colleagues. Congressmen had joked and snickered for years about Yvette and Corrine.

But the Hays committee's private investigators began uncovering things that were not common knowledge. For instance, on August 1, 1966, Powell had hired a young woman named Sylvia J. Givens as a secretary. He had promptly outfitted her with uniforms and had told her to go work as a maid at a house he had bought in the Bahamas. The committee also discovered that Powell had charged scores of airline tickets for flights between New York, Washington, D.C., and Miami, Florida, to the account of

his office staff, supposedly for congressional business. Yet the tickets had really been used by Powell and Corrine Huff. An office receptionist was listed as having made 30 trips at the government's expense, but she acknowledged to the committee that she had used the tickets herself only 3 times.

Where was Powell? As Hays and his committee pored through his affairs in the fall of 1966, the congressman appeared to be having the time of his life. Unable to go to New York without risking arrest, not on speaking terms with Yvette in Puerto Rico, constantly criticized by his political colleagues, Powell headed for Bimini, a sun-drenched island in the Bahamas, just off the coast of Florida.

Bimini has been called an "uncut little jewel" and is still famous mainly for its spectacular deep-sea fishing. A devoted fisherman, Powell first sailed there in 1963. Enchanted by Bimini, he built a two-bedroom house on the island and soon began spending more time there and less in Washington, D.C. For Bimini's mostly black population, Powell was an uncrowned king. Again and again, visitors were told, "Adam Clayton Powell is the greatest man in the world." A journalist said, "It's a line that seems to be used on Bimini whenever there is a lull in conversation, the equivalent of clearing one's throat."

Powell's presence had greatly changed the atmosphere on Bimini, and the islanders had much to be grateful for. Powell had not only broken the color line—prior to his arrival, restaurants and clubs were for whites only—but his fame brought Bimini a glare of publicity beyond a travel agent's wildest dreams. As his troubles back home mounted, reporters, broadcasters, and photographers trooped back and forth in the blazing sun, hoping for a word from him.

The media people knew that on most days there were two places to see Powell: at the pier in the morning and at the End of the World bar in the

afternoon. He and Corrine Huff were inseparable, and each morning at 10:30 or 11:00 they would board his boat, "Adam's Fancy," and roar out to sea. They would leave the dock earlier when there was a fishing tournament, for Powell's considerable skill with a rod and line enabled him to grab most of the trophies. After three or four hours of fishing, the boat would cruise home, and Powell would retire to the ram-shackle, weather-beaten End of the World bar for an afternoon of domino playing and uncounted rounds of the favorite local drink, Scotch and milk.

In this languid paradise Powell found it hard to pay much attention to events in Washington, D.C. In January 1967, he flew to the capital for the opening of Congress. As he sauntered into his office, he casually asked Chuck Stone, his administrative assistant, "What's up, baby?"

"What's up?" Stone yelled back. "You're gonna lose your seat, that's what!"

As Powell's political fortunes declined in the late 1960s, he began to spend an increasing amount of time at his retreat in Bimini, an island in the Bahamas.

A group of civil rights activists pickets the White House to protest the impending censure of Powell by Congress. The Harlem congressman insisted that he was a victim of racial discrimination.

It finally dawned on Powell how precarious things had become for him. Armed with the findings of the Hays committee, the Democrats in the House met on January 9, 1967, and voted to strip him of his chairmanship of the Committee on Education and Labor. After the vote, Powell's hands trembled as he talked with reporters and described the vote as "a lynching—Northern style."

The following day, Morris "Mo" Udall, a tall, genial representative from Arizona, stood in a House chamber doing a job he would just as soon have avoided—trying to save Powell's job. The Harlem congressman's indiscretions—the legal fiasco with Esther James, the spectacular junkets abroad, the abuse of his congressional payroll, his arrogance—had finally come home to roost. Nearly every congressman agreed that something had to be done about him. Unless Powell was disciplined severely, they argued, the House would be the laughingstock of the country. The Republicans, and more than a few Democrats, wanted to deny him his seat, first, and then inquire into his misconduct. Udall was the closest to an ally that Powell had. He argued for a resolution authorizing an investigation but permitting Powell to take the oath of office and his seat in the House.

Powell walked in as the debate began. Heads turned to catch a glimpse of the tall, tanned New Yorker in a well-cut blue suit as he ambled down the center aisle. He approached Udall and asked if he could speak on behalf of the resolution. Udall hesitated. An unrepentant Powell would do no good. But, Udall said, if Powell was contrite, then his speaking would help. Powell retreated to a seat and hastily scribbled a short speech on a yellow legal pad. He then showed what he had written to Udall. It was mildly conciliatory. The Arizonan smiled and said, "That's fine, Adam. I'll save the last five minutes for you."

When Powell's time to speak arrived, the House grew very quiet. At the rostrum, just in front of the

Speaker's table, Powell removed his glasses and deliberately pushed aside the yellow sheet of paper, ignoring it completely. "My beloved colleagues," he began in a sarcastic tone. Udall groaned, thinking that he should have known that an apology was not in Powell's vocabulary. "I know this is an agonizing moment for you," Powell continued. "I know if you could vote on a secret ballot, your vote would be different from what you have proclaimed publicly, because you know I have been here 23 years and he who is without sin should cast the first stone. There is no one here who does not have a skeleton in his closet. I know, and I know them by name."

When Powell's five minutes were up, he concluded: "Gentlemen, my conscience is clean. My case is in God's hands. All I hope is that you have a good sleep tonight." On his way from the rostrum, he stopped beside Udall and said, "We both did what we had to do, Mo."

After Powell was denied his congressional seat, a special House committee was established to determine his fitness to serve. He is shown here testifying before the investigative committee.

Congressman Emanuel Celler, a friend of Powell's as well as a fellow New York Democrat, headed the special House committee inquiring into Powell's transgressions as an elected official.

Powell stood at the rear of the chamber long enough to get a sense of the roll call on the resolution. His "beloved colleagues" were trampling one another in the rush to vote against him. On the final tally, only 65 representatives voted for Udall's resolution, while 363 said Powell should not have a seat.

On the steps outside the Capitol, a crowd was waiting for Powell. Nearly all of the people in the crowd were black and angry. Powell spoke to them, ungratefully cursing Udall and then gesturing to the Capitol with his cigar and declaring, "This building houses the biggest bunch of elected hypocrites in the world." But Powell was without a seat, and Harlem was without a congressman.

Powell's expulsion from the House was not expected to be permanent. A special committee, headed by Powell's friend Emanuel Celler of New York, was set up by the House to investigate Powell's misconduct. At the conclusion of its inquiry, the committee was supposed to report back to the House and suggest a final resolution of Powell's status. It was widely assumed that the committee would recommend that he be censured and fined but allowed to assume his seat.

At the special committee's first public hearing, Powell testified briefly. His words were defiant, but his manner had lost the old swagger. Andrew Jacobs of Indiana, a committee member, was surprised by the change. "For the first time," Jacobs said, "he looked his 58 years. There were wrinkles on his forehead. The phenomenon of his perpetual youth seemed to have drained away. For all his so-called bravado I detected apprehension. The clothes were still stylish, but the shoulders sagged ever so slightly."

Powell put up a brave front, but his colleagues had wounded him badly. He loved being a congressman and a committee chairman. In his unorthodox way, he loved the House and its traditions. Now, even if he should reclaim his seat, it could never again be the same for him in Congress.

Powell was back in Bimini when the next dagger came flying. His wife, Yvette, appeared before the special committee and testified about her husband's transgressions. Powell was deeply hurt. "I never thought the day would come when Yvette would turn on me," he said.

Yvette's action should not have surprised Powell. He was by no means a devoted husband. The previous August, Yvette had come to Washington, D.C., bringing along four-year-old Adamcito. They checked into the Sheraton Park Hotel and called Powell's office. He refused to see her or his son. After hanging up on her, he promptly called the hotel's manager and said under no circumstances were his wife's bills to be sent to him. A few days later, miserable and alone in the city, Yvette and Adamcito returned to Puerto Rico.

Appearing before the committee, Yvette seemed nervous and timid as she described her position on the Powell staff payroll. In the early 1960s, she had indeed translated letters from her husband's Spanish-speaking constituents, and she believed she was performing a full-time job. However, the bundles of letters had stopped coming by 1965, and so had Powell.

Amazingly, in six years Yvette had received only four paychecks. "I'll take care of the finances," Powell said after they were married, and he was good to his word. Even though Yvette had never given him the authority to sign her name, Powell endorsed her payroll checks himself. Nearly all the checks bore the notation "For Deposit Only to the Account of Hon. Adam C. Powell."

In March 1967, the special committee concluded its work and reported to the House. As expected, it recommended that Powell be admitted as a member but that he endure some severe punishment. He would

When Powell's wife Yvette appeared before the special House committee, she gave damaging evidence against her estranged husband, testifying that she had not done any work for him in more than a year and a half even though she was still on his congressional payroll.

be stripped of all seniority, fined $40,000, and publicly censured for "gross misconduct."

The committee's recommendation was not approved. The House heard the Powell report, "with blood in our nostrils," according to one member. One after another, indignant representatives said that the committee's suggestion was too soft. They demanded that Powell be thrown out of Congress. He had violated "one of the Ten Commandments, 'Thou shalt not steal,' " intoned one Republican congressman. Powell's opponents had their way. By a final vote of 307 to 116, Powell was expelled from the House, thereby joining a socialist, a polygamist, and a seller of military academy appointments as the only representatives in history to be denied the seats they had won at the polls.

The expulsion was without constitutional foundation. The House had every right in the world to discipline Powell, to take away his seniority, his chairmanship, his office, even his parking space, but to exclude him from Congress denied the 450,000 residents of Harlem their right to select whomever they wanted to represent them in Washington. After the vote, the chairman of the special committee said

After Powell was removed from his seat in Congress, he filed a legal suit against the House of Representatives, claiming that his expulsion was unconstitutional. During this legal battle, he spent most of his time in Bimini.

glumly, "If I were representing Adam Clayton Powell, I'd take the case to court right away. I think he's got a good case."

Powell wasted no time in mounting his appeal. Represented by a team of constitutional lawyers, he filed suit against the House. The case began to work its way through the courts, but in the meantime Powell was left out in the cold, a congressman without a seat. However, in the days after his expulsion, he rediscovered friends he thought he had lost. Black leaders rallied to his side. Martin Luther King, Jr., said that the House action was racist. Whitney Young of the National Urban League agreed. A leader of the Congress of Racial Equality called the House decision "a slap in the face of every black man in this country."

Powell received the news of the House action calmly, at the End of the World bar in Bimini. Sipping a Scotch and milk, occasionally diverted by an exotic dancer, he fielded questions from the press. When asked if he would run for Congress again, he said, "That depends upon my good people in Harlem. I wouldn't deny my people. I'll do anything my people want me to do."

Harlem still supported Powell. A special election was called to fill his now-vacant seat, and Powell was the only man the voters would hear of. On April 11, 1967, he was triumphantly reelected, gaining 28,000 votes to 4,000 for his nearest opponent.

Most of the people voting for Powell expected him to reappear in Washington, D.C., and renew the battle with the House. After all, he had never been one to walk away from a fight. But this time, he did not even present his certificate of election to the House clerk. Preferring the long process of legal appeal, he stayed in Bimini, falling deeper and deeper into a pit of despair. His seat in Congress remained empty. ◖◗

8

THE LAST HURRAH

❧

AFTER POWELL'S STIRRING victory in the special election of 1967, when he stayed in Bimini rather than try to reclaim his seat, things continued to turn sour. Corrine Huff walked out on him and married the captain of his fishing boat. A large part of his assets were in her name and went with her. Severely depressed, Powell started drinking heavily, no longer the sociable Scotch and milk but vodka and Tang. He sometimes drank straight vodka, as much as a quart a day.

In 1968, he briefly roused himself from this torpor and arranged to settle the Esther James case. Using proceeds from the sale of an album, "Keep the Faith, Baby!" a recording of his sermons, he began paying the damages that he owed James. This permitted him to return to New York without fear of arrest, and on March 22, 1968, he made a dramatic reappearance in Harlem.

Hearing that he was back, a crowd spontaneously gathered along Seventh Avenue, happily shouting "Keep the faith, baby," and "Fight, baby, fight." On the following Sunday, he preached for the first time in years at Abyssinia. He was more militant and angry than he had ever been in the pulpit, and he called

Powell returned to Harlem in March 1968 after staying away from his congressional district for nearly two years. A settlement in the Esther James's slander case made it legally possible for him to return to New York.

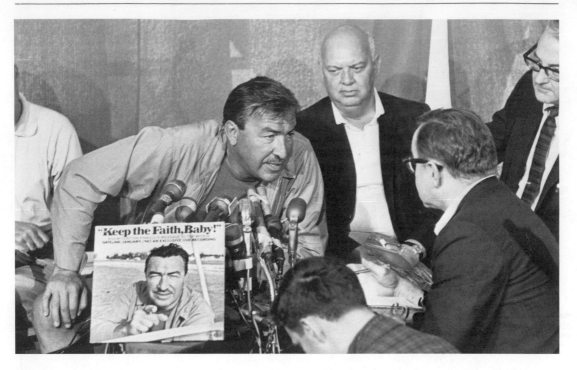

Powell used the money that he earned from "Keep the Faith, Baby!" (a record album of his sermons) to pay Esther James for the damages that he had caused her by slandering her character.

for revolution. Blacks, he said, must "lead the revolution with any white people who will follow us as troops. And if this doesn't happen black Africans and colored people of Asia and South America will rise up against the United States."

His speeches fell flat. After the excitement of his return had worn off, Harlem took a hard look at its idol and found him wanting. His militancy—he embraced some of the most radical black-nationalist groups in Harlem and criticized nonviolence—shocked many in the community. He also looked as though his long years of hard living had caught up with him. A spectator to this last hurrah wrote, "His once gleaming black hair was streaked with gray, his face was deeply lined and puffy, the flesh hanging loosely from his jowls. Even his clothes seemed a bit seedy and mismatched."

In the 1968 elections, Powell won a 13th term in Congress, but by a shockingly small margin over a little-known foe. The temper of the House had cooled down by January 1969, and Powell was allowed to take his seat, although the appeal of his previous expulsion was still being reviewed by the Supreme Court. However, his colleagues fined him $25,000, which was to be deducted from his paychecks, and took away all his seniority. By then, he was only going through the motions. In the 1969 session, he answered only 9 of 177 roll calls and spent most days in Bimini.

On June 16, 1969, the Supreme Court finally ruled on Powell's appeal of his 1967 expulsion from Congress. In a 7 to 1 decision, the Court ruled in Powell's favor. Writing his last decision as chief justice, Earl Warren said that in the view of the Court, "the House was without power to exclude him from membership."

Powell hardly felt like celebrating his victory, for he was a desperately ill man. In the summer of 1969, his doctors diagnosed a malignancy in his lymphatic system, and its treatment required painful cobalt therapy. His health began to deteriorate daily.

During the spring of 1970, Powell was in the last political fight of his life. At a street corner in Harlem, he began speaking to a small crowd. Just as he hit his stride, a young man interrupted him.

"Mr. Powell, you gonna be at our narcotics parade next Saturday like you promised?" the young man asked.

"Sure, sure," Powell said, and he began to talk about his 40 years of service to Harlem. A minute later, the youth again asked if he were coming to the parade. Annoyed, Powell snapped, "I wouldn't miss it if my life depended on it."

A moment afterward, the young man piped up once more. "Well, Mr. Powell, sir," he said, "you ain't gonna be there Saturday, 'cause there ain't no parade and we never spoke about one."

His political career over and his health declining, Powell departed from the public eye in 1970.

Funeral services for Powell were held at the Abyssinian Baptist Church on April 9, 1972. As both a minister and a politician, he left a striking legacy of black solidarity.

Away from Harlem for so long, Powell was badly out of touch with events and conditions in his district. While he was driving uptown, a car full of young men stopped beside him at a traffic light. The young men stared at the car, then at the driver. "It's Adam Powell!" one said. "I thought you was dead!"

Politically, he was. In the Democratic primary on June 23, 1970, Harlem—Powell's loyal, faithful, unswerving Harlem—turned against him. By the narrowest of margins, the voters selected State Assemblyman Charles Rangel for Congress, not Adam Clayton Powell, a dying legend.

After his defeat, Powell went once more to Bimini, to sit in the sun with his last mistress, a young woman from Mississippi named Darlene Exposé, and to dictate his memoirs into a tape recorder. He died on April 4, 1972, after an emergency operation in Miami.

Powell's body was returned to Harlem for services at Abyssinia. "I am what I am because of the Abyssinian Church," he had once said. At his funeral, all of his last years of humiliation and despondency seemed to have been cast away from him, and he was once again remembered as the dynamic young Harlem minister and defiant congressman. Thousands stood in long lines to pass by his casket. The great stone church was filled with the famous, the infamous, and the unknown.

Surely, only a few that day could look to the pulpit and not see Adam Clayton Powell there, his tall, strong body swaying beneath a flowing black robe trimmed with crimson braid, his magnificent voice rising and falling, his arms gesturing dramatically. The faithful could see their minister, their congressman, their champion, step from the marble pulpit as he did each Sunday after the sermon and come to stand in the center aisle of the church. His arms would be spread wide, his head tilted back, his voice soft and forgiving as he asked all who were not church members to come forward and take his hand. "What are you holding back for? Why not put your hand in mine and join the assembly of God?" ◆

CHRONOLOGY

Nov. 29, 1908   Born Adam Clayton Powell, Jr., in New Haven, Connecticut

1908   Family moves to Harlem

1925   Graduates from Townsend Harris High School; enters City College of New York

1926   Sister, Blanche, dies; Powell enters Colgate University

1930   Graduates from Colgate; enters the Teachers College of Columbia University; becomes assistant minister and business manager of Abyssinia

1932   Graduates from Columbia with a master's degree in theological studies

1933   Marries Isabel Washington

1938   Organizes the Greater New York Coordinating Committee on Employment

1941   Is elected to the New York City Council

1944   Is elected to the House of Representatives

1945   Marries Hazel Scott

1946   First son, Adam Clayton Powell III, is born; Powell introduces the Powell amendment

1952   Is investigated by the Justice Department and the Internal Revenue Service

1958   Is indicted for tax evasion

1960   Marries Yvette Marjorie Flores Diago

1961   Becomes the chairman of the Committee on Education and Labor

1962   Second son, Adam Clayton Powell-Diago, is born

1967   Powell is expelled from Congress

1969   Returns to Congress

1970   Fails to be reelected to Congress

April 4, 1972   Dies in Miami, Florida

FURTHER READING

————— ❧ —————

Hapwood, David. *The Purge That Failed: Tammany Against Powell*. New York: Holt, Rinehart & Winston, 1959.

Haskins, James. *Adam Clayton Powell: Portrait of a Marching Black*. New York: Dial Press, 1974.

Jacobs, Andy. *The Powell Affair: Freedom Minus One*. Indianapolis: Bobbs-Merrill, 1973.

Kilson, Martin. "Adam Clayton Powell, Jr.: The Militant as Politician." In *Black Leaders of the Twentieth Century*, edited by John Hope Franklin and August Meier. Urbana: University of Illinois Press, 1982.

Lewis, Claude. *Adam Clayton Powell*. Greenwich, CT: Fawcett, 1963.

Powell, Adam Clayton, Jr. *Adam by Adam*. New York: Dial Press, 1971.

———. *Keep the Faith, Baby!* New York: Trident Press, 1967.

———. *Marching Blacks*. New York: Dial Press, 1945; rev. ed., 1973.

Weeks, Kent M. *Adam Clayton Powell and the Supreme Court*. New York: Dunellen, 1971.

INDEX

PICTURE CREDITS

ROBERT E. JAKOUBEK is coauthor of *These United States,* an American history textbook. A native of Iowa, he now lives in New York City.

NATHAN IRVIN HUGGINS is W.E.B. Du Bois Professor of History and Director of the W.E.B. Du Bois Institute for Afro-American Research at Harvard University. He previously taught at Columbia University. Professor Huggins is the author of numerous books, including *Black Odyssey: The Afro-American Ordeal in Slavery, The Harlem Renaissance,* and *Slave and Citizen: The Life of Frederick Douglass.*